Double Take

Bill Brodie

Copyright © 2015 Bill Brodie

All rights reserved.

ISBN – 13:978-1505876826

DEDICATION

Next to my faith, my family are the most precious gift God
could have given me in this world.
I happily dedicate this book to them.

CONTENTS

Introduction	6
Part 1 – Revelation from Above	7
Look at the sky…	8
Count the stars if you can	11
Strange things you might hear in church	15
(1) The message of Creation was not clear enough to convert people	16
(2) The Old Testament saints did not have the same faith in Christ as New Testament believers	21
(3) The Spirit of God was *on* Old Testament believers but not *in* them	29
Meditations	43
Why does God not appear more often?	44
Consider the Flowers of the Field	46

Wouldn't it be nice?...   48

Part 2 – Children of the Living God   50

Children of the Living God   51

Why are we so often down on ourselves?   55

    (1) Wrong perspectives on man's place in the universe   56

    (2) Exaggerating the difference between God and man   59

    (3) An over-emphasis on being "sinners"   62

Meditations   69

    Sculpted to Perfection   70

    The Family Business. Why is prayer so important?   72

    The Painting   75

Part 3 – Double Take 77

Being Made Righteous 78

You Have Heard It Said… 84

   (1) Forgiveness 85

   (2) Declarative Righteousness 93

   (3) Proof-Texts and Fantasies 101

   (4) "New" Perspectives on Paul 118

   (5) "Justification" and "Sanctification" 124

   (6) Romans 7 – The Controversial "Man" 128

Meditations 145

   Heart Transplant 146

   Postcard from Israel - The Beauty of Holiness 148

The Light from Behind the Sun	150

Part 4 – Bringing Many Sons To Glory — 152

A Glorious Future	153
Hope – A Marginalized Teaching	164
Difficult Texts	171
Romans 5:3-5. Character and Hope	172
2 Corinthians 5:1-7. Bodiless?	175
Matthew 24:40-41. "Rapture?"	179

Meditations — 186

Meeting Your Maker	187
Home Movies	189
Heavenly Perspectives	193

Part 5 – Contentment   195

Daily Contentment: Enjoy the Moment   196

Meditations   205

    Kisses from God   206

    Can we praise God while the world falls apart?   208

    Family Holiday   213

References and Further Reading   216

A Bio Postscript from the Author   220

Introduction

Let me offer a quick word of introduction about what kind of reading experience you might expect to find in this book.

Firstly, I have to say that I have the sort of mind that doesn't like loose ends. So I have written the kind of book that I would like to read myself. I've asked a range of difficult questions, and I've answered them – in ways that I think make sense.

I know there are many people like me whose faith doesn't depend on having all the answers; but we get distracted if we hear theology creaking, and we find doctrinal anomalies an irritant. So we keep questioning.

Equally, I know many people who are not bothered at all by doctrinal complexities. Their Christian zeal and love are driven by a grasp of core principles and they are not easily distracted by conundrums. I admire that. In your case you may prefer to go straight to the meditations at the end of each of the book's five sections and enjoy some moments of reflection.

For all types of readers, the contents list should prove a useful navigation aid so that the book can be used as a sort of reference manual which you can dip into from time to time as things cross your mind.

This is a controversial book, but I hope, a helpful one. I pray for a heart-warming blessing on everyone who picks it up.

Bill Brodie, Jan 2015

PART 1

REVELATION FROM ABOVE

"Look at the sky..."

The heavens declare the glory of God, and the sky above proclaims his handiwork. Day to day pours out speech, and night to night reveals knowledge.
There is no speech, nor are there words, whose voice is not heard. Their voice goes out through all the earth, and their words to the end of the world.[1]

When we look up into the skies, by day or at night, our hearts should be drawn into the presence of the invisible deity whose power and genius have given substance to this breathtaking creation. We should sense him – dazzling and awesome – behind, above, and through it all.

The natural human response, then, should be to begin to feel after this great Creator; to try to find out more about him; to pray and want to contact him.

We should feel the same stirrings of worship in our hearts when we see the miracle of a new human life coming "fearfully and wonderfully made" out of a mother's womb;[2]

---

[1] Psalm 19:1-4

[2] *"...the human body bears on its face such proofs of ingenious contrivance as are sufficient to proclaim the admirable wisdom of its Maker."* Jean Calvin, Institutes of the Christian Religion, Trans. Henry Beveridge (1949), Vol 1, p 52.

or when the scientist gazes down his microscope at myriads of intricate worlds; or when we find ourselves entranced by the sheer brilliance of plant and animal life around us.

Instead, most human beings see and sense nothing of the beautiful creator. If they do, now and then, and something mystical stirs within them, they don't pursue it. They don't want to find out about him. They are not interested in a life of worship.

This is our perverse nature – our fallen human default.

Paul the Apostle taught that this human blindness is deliberate.[3] It is our inborn aversion to living a life with God at its centre. We have no taste for it – no desire for the religious walk. This natural hardness of heart can only be changed when God touches us and gives us the faith that accepts him as the source of all life and blessing (Hebrews 11:3,6).

By faith we understand.

Then we see that all good things come from him (James 1:17). We embark on a life of thanksgiving and willing devotion, knowing that he is a generous and a powerful God, who delights to bless, to help, and restore.

Human beings can know these truths about God even before they hear the detailed "gospel" message of God's plan of blessing through the death and resurrection of Jesus

---

[3] Romans 1:18-21.

Christ.

We can have saving faith before we have heard all the exact New Testament doctrines.[4] It is a faith, above all, which puts us into a proper relationship with God the Creator.

The whole Bible, from Genesis to Revelation, is about the relationship between God and the family he longs to bless. Faith sees him for who he is and is the basis for receiving and giving love – the overriding motivation in everything he ever plans and does.

---

[4] See the example of Apollos in Acts 18.

"Count the stars, if you can"

That is the sort of faith that Abraham had when he first received God's promises about future blessings – and later when he was tested about Isaac. He believed that God had great rewards in store for him and many others. He trusted God's word that the birth of an heir would lead to the inheritance of a blessed land – on earth first and then in heaven.[5]

Abraham's faith was a saving faith. Faith in itself doesn't save anyone, but it connects us to the source of life and blessing. It enables us to say yes to God's power; it opens our arms to accept his solutions to the evils that stand in the way of our happiness – sin and death.

This was the faith God tested in Abraham when he was asked to sacrifice Isaac. God's promises, and Abraham's entire understanding of God's goodness, were tied up with the life of that son. As Calvin puts it so well:

" Isaac was the mirror of eternal life, and the pledge of

---

[5] Calvin explains how belief in a specific promise is inextricably bound up with faith in God's goodness in general and with all his interlinked promises: "...*the believing of which Moses speaks, is not to be restricted to a single clause of the promise here referred to, but embraces the whole...this promise was not taken by him separately from others.... It is indeed to be maintained as an axiom that all the promises of God made to the faithful...are evidences of that paternal love, and of that gratuitous adoption, on which their salvation is founded.*" The Geneva Series of Commentaries. Genesis (1984). Trans. J. King. pp 406-407.

all good things."[6]

Abraham passed the test with flying colours – as he had done at every stage in his journey with God.[7] He believed that even death, couldn't stop God fulfilling his promises of blessing for him and for the world. If it meant resurrection – God could do even that. Blessing by a resurrection was therefore what Abraham and his descendants received – and receive still – through faith.

Abraham's faith is held out to all believers ever since, under the Old and the New Testament, as our model. When we trust God for blessings, he makes us righteous. There can be no life, no glory, no inheritance without a restored relationship with him. But God has done all that is necessary through Christ to restore us to himself and a life of blessing. When we trust him, that salvation is what we get. In the end, it is not faith in doctrinal promises that saves us, but faith in a person – God as our loving Father.

> "Therefore we do not say that Abram was justified because he laid hold on a single word, respecting the offspring... but because he embraced God as his Father."[8]

* * * * * * * * * * * * *

---

6. Ibid p 565.

7. Hebrews 11:8-19 makes it clear that his redeeming faith was a lifelong one, not restricted to one incident, though exemplified memorably in particular episodes.

[8] Calvin: Genesis, p 407.

My own pre-Christian experience began with early emotional stirrings around Christmas time, as I gazed at the moving nativity story pictured on Christmas cards and looked for it in old Bibles; then years later during solitary teenage walks, as I began to sense that there may be some supernatural presence "out there". Around that time, by chance I overheard a school friend telling others about the great happiness which God could give to people. One evening, on impulse, I knelt and asked that if God was there, he would give me that happy experience.

Not much saving theology there, you might think! But God saw that I had the sort of faith described by the writer of Hebrews as pleasing to him,[9] and he rushed towards me with an infilling of his Spirit that meant my life was changed overnight – and forever.

Knowledge of all the key doctrines quickly followed. And not for a minute in my Christian life have I doubted any of them – though I confess I have not always lived up to them as well as I would have wished.

* * * * * * * * * * * * *

The relationship between faith, doctrine and revelation requires careful thought. It raises the question, among others, whether there is hope for people who never hear the full "gospel" of Jesus Christ – for example those living in

---

[9] *Whoever would draw near to God must believe that he is and that he is a rewarder of those who seek him.* Hebrews 11:6.

remote tribes, or growing up in deeply Islamic societies. Can they meet God in nature around them? Can they find him in the stars?

At the same time, it raises questions about faith and experience during the Old Testament period, compared to our modern knowledge of the Christian Good News. Could Old Testament believers have the same experience of salvation as we now enjoy, without having the detailed story of Jesus' life and death?

This is such a difficult area that many church leaders have ended up thinking themselves into very strange doctrinal positions....

The challenge, I think, is like trying to do a 1,000-piece jigsaw. When you look at a certain bit of scripture, you may be sure that it fits into another, because the join seems to be an obvious one. But unless you keep an eye on the big picture, you can end up working from a misguided starting point. Increasingly you will find yourself having to force things together that don't fit. The picture you are left with in the end will be full of gaps – and inevitably bizarre.

In the following section we will explore some of these issues.

Then in the final section of this Part we offer a few devotional meditations on these themes.

Strange Things You Might Hear in Church

(1) The message of Creation was not clear enough to convert people

(2) The Old Testament saints did not have the same faith in Christ as New Testament believers

(3) The Spirit of God was *on* Old Testament believers but not *in* them

Strange things...

(1) The message of Creation was not clear enough to convert people

It's sometimes said that there was not a worldwide turning to God before the Christian gospel was preached because the message of God in creation was never clear enough. That's why it couldn't (and still can't) save people in the way that the gospel does.

This needs to be thought through carefully.

Firstly we must be in no doubt about what Paul says – that the truth about God was *always* clear enough in Creation to leave the world's inhabitants no excuse for not finding and knowing him. The problem, according to Paul, was not a lack of clarity – but the hardness of human hearts.[10]

If any man or woman ever genuinely began to "feel after" God, inspired by the vision of creation around them, there is no doubt that God would more than meet them half way. God will eagerly reach out to those who are trying to find him – as he did so spectacularly in the case of the Ethiopian Eunuch (Acts 8). And still today, many Arab Christians are

---

[10] Romans 1:18-32.

reported to have been converted through special visitations by God in dreams, and unexpected visions of Christ.

On the other hand many people *appear* to be seeking God via a monotheistic faith, such as Islam. But it is hard to see them as genuine seekers of God if they continue to resist the core message that comes from God – salvation through Jesus Christ. If these people were spiritual, would the divine Spirit not make it a priority to convince them of the truths about the very Son of God?

There are some doctrines which people may be wrong about, or ill-informed, and still be true believers. But the central truths of Jesus' life, mission, death and resurrection are surely essential to any real faith.

Based on Paul's assessment of the global ignorance of God (Romans 1), we can say that if people anywhere are stuck in ignorance, they are "without excuse". The corollary is also true: even remote tribes who have not heard the gospel, or those born into cultures dominated by false religions, can and will come to know God through Jesus Christ if they are true seekers.

Calvin is right of course when he says in his "Institutes" that the latter-day, scriptural message of the gospel of Christ was necessary to *complete* the revelation of God in nature,[11]

---

[11] *Therefore, while it becomes man seriously to employ his eyes in considering the works of God... in this most glorious theatre..., his special duty is to give ear to the Word, that he may the better profit.* Institutes. Vol 1, p 66.

to give mankind a fuller picture. He also states that the gospel of the scriptures preached worldwide was necessary because the revelation of God in nature was generally not effective in bringing people to a saving knowledge if God.[12]

We just need to be careful about mixing up these two issues and falling into a logic trap about *why* gospel preaching works, while a revelation of God through creation so often doesn't. We cannot simply correlate clarity with effectiveness.

It is, rather, a question of God's sovereignty – in timing and in method.

At the right time in history, God the Father authorized the preaching of the Good News of Jesus Christ as his main way of spreading knowledge of his grace worldwide. This has been his normal means of reaching out to a lost mankind. It has meant salvation for millions of people since Jesus' death and resurrection.

But this ministry of the Good News has been effective not just because it is clearer or more complete. It is clearer. It is more complete. But it is effective because it is God's chosen way to reach out to people across the earth and adopt them into his heavenly family.

---

[12] *God, foreseeing the inefficiency of his image imprinted in the fair form of the universe, has given the assistance of his Word to all whom he has ever been pleased to instruct...* (Ibid p 66).

The timing also was in his sovereign choice. Paul talks about the mystery of Christ (Ephesians 3:1-11) which was *not* made known "to the sons of men in other generations" as it was revealed to him and the other Apostles for spreading around the world at that time in history – with the result, he says, that even Gentiles would become joint-heirs in the gospel of grace.[13]

The Israelites, as the chosen people, had already been given the privilege of seeing the day of Christ coming, though they may have been more or less sure about the details. The other nations (Gentiles) were left in darkness until then. But even in their case, Paul says that the message of God written in Creation had always been clear enough to leave people without excuse. God had never left himself without a witness (Acts 14:17). Human blindness, says Paul, is wilful.

When God left people in ignorance, waiting for the right time to spread the word of Christ, this was their choice as much as his. Debate has raged over the centuries as to whether salvation is dependent on man's free will or on God's sovereign choice. My answer is that when we find two opposite extremes declared authoritatively in the scriptures,

---

[13] Translators get hold of the wrong end of the stick in this passage when they see the inclusion of the Gentiles as the "mystery" which Paul says had been hidden (RSV, NRSV, NIV). The *mystery* is salvation through Jesus. The Gentiles' blessing was the *purpose* and *result* of this revelation (verse 6: εἶναι) – not the mystery itself.

we should believe both equally. In heaven we will know how that paradox can be true.

The word of Christ was God's means of spreading his light around the world in an historically unprecedented way. The Good News spread globally beyond Israel. It was a fuller, clearer word than the message he had left for mankind in his Creation. Yet in exactly the same way as nations had wilfully refused to see God's glory in creation, millions of people today still turn their back on the clear gospel message because they simply won't accept it.

It is not the clarity of the message or otherwise that is the final issue. As Jesus said, even if someone rose from the dead before people's very eyes, many would not believe.[14]

We need to remember this when we are sharing the Good News with others. We must always try to make our message as clear and convincing as we can.[15] But at the end of the day, people have a free choice – and some will prefer the darkness of life without God.

---

[14] Luke 16:31.

[15] 1 Peter 3:15.

Strange things...

(2). The Old Testament saints did not have the same faith in Christ as New Testament believers

This is another tricky question that can easily prompt people to hasty, ill-informed conclusions. What revelation of the truth did the saints of the Old Testament period have?

It is important to emphasize that there has only ever been *one* way of salvation taught throughout the whole Bible. It is the same saving grace offered by God whether in the Old Testament or in the New. The expression of it may be different, but the heart of it has always been the same.

There are scriptures which seem to suggest that a new "gospel" has replaced an old, malfunctioning covenant; that one is effective in giving spiritual life, while the other could never save. But this needs to be examined very carefully.

If we can get beyond superficial impressions created by certain "proof-texts", we see that there has always been *one* gospel of salvation by grace, through faith alone. Even when it says that "The Law was given through Moses; grace and truth came through Jesus Christ," we must understand that *grace and truth* were on offer all along – long before Jesus came. The life and death of Jesus work backwards in time for men's salvation, as well as forwards for us. Men and women of faith – whether in Moses' time or in the present day – have always believed that salvation is a free gift of God.

We see this clearly in the way Paul writes about Abraham's belief. The Patriarch's faith was the same faith that he wants us to have (Romans 4:1-25). Paul makes no distinction between Abraham's faith, righteousness or share in God's blessings and ours.

We are told that Abraham's reward for his righteousness through faith was the future inheritance of the earth. In the context of earthly life, that meant firstly the blessings of the land that would be Israel. But Abraham knew that this was only the beginning – a sign and a foretaste of heavenly blessings.[16] Enjoyment of life in that promised land would point to eternal citizenship in a new, glorious earth crowned with its heavenly Zion. He believed both in an earthly blessing and heavenly salvation. They were inseparably linked.

Some Bible teachers maintain that Old Testament saints had no belief in the resurrection nor in heaven's rewards; that they focused only on God's material blessings in this life. This is doing them a great injustice! Read the inspiring

---

[16] *These temporal blessings did not constitute an end in themselves, but served to symbolize and typify spiritual and heavenly blessings.* Berkhof, Systematic Theology, (1941 reprinted 1988), p 296.

list of "heroes of faith"[17] in Hebrews 11. It is clear that they all had a compelling vision of eternal blessings – no matter how much this was also linked to God's promises for Israel's land and its temporal blessings.

> **"For people who speak thus make it clear that they are seeking a homeland... they desire a better country, that is, a heavenly one. Therefore God is not ashamed to be called their God, for he has prepared for them a city."[18]**

Hebrews 11 shows that all the listed heroes of faith shared our faith as the channel of saving righteousness (Hebrews 11:4,5,7). Linked with this was their assurance that they would receive heavenly blessings on the basis of that righteousness (Hebrews 11:10,13,16,26). The writer shows that Faith and Hope go inseparably together: most of the blessings we believe for, are awaiting future fulfilment.

So what does the writer of Hebrews mean when he says that these men and women of faith died without receiving "what was promised because God had foreseen something better for us, that apart from us they should not be made perfect" (Hebrews 11:39-40)? Is he implying a two-tier programme of blessing? Do we get a better offer than them?

---

[17] The title of a series of studies based on Hebrews 11 by the late Rev William Still of Gilcomston South Church, Aberdeen.

[18] Hebrews 11:14-16.

Was their package of blessings inferior to ours?

The writer is referring there to the future blessings of heaven, as he has been doing throughout that 11th chapter. The Old Testament believers lived in hope of heavenly rewards. They haven't attained these yet through resurrection (i.e. they haven't been "made perfect") because God wanted future generations, including us, to benefit also from his salvation. So the Old Testament saints haven't yet attained their rewards. God didn't want the story to end too soon. This is the meaning of "God had foreseen something better for us". We were going to be included. It's not that our blessings would be better than theirs.

Our hope of eternal life and glory is based on our clear knowledge of the death and resurrection of Jesus Christ. We have the apostolic scriptures and access to the full account. So how enlightened could those Old Testament saints have been about the "gospel" of Jesus?

When we read 1 Peter 1:10-12 about the prophets of old, it is tempting to focus on what they didn't know (the exact time and human identity of the promised Messiah[19]). But we shouldn't overlook the fact that they were even then prophesying a message of salvation by grace through the Messiah – during the period of Old Testament Law.

---

[19] Cf. Luke 10:24.

Equally, when it says these prophets realized they were serving us (latter-day saints) and not themselves, we should not read into this that they personally were unable to benefit from grace, whereas we do. It means simply, they realized that the full clarity of the wonderful story was to be kept for later generations. It was not going to be made available to them in detail at that stage.

But those prophets – and all believers in the Old Testament period – had enough knowledge of the message of grace to believe it, along with us, and to attain the same righteousness with its promised rewards.

The Old Testament scriptures from the beginning were full of the message of Christ. Spiritual people always saw this. Salvation by grace was there all along for believers with eyes of faith.

This is why Jesus was able to show the continuity of his message throughout all the Hebrew scriptures.[20]

> **"And beginning with Moses and all the prophets, he interpreted to them in all the scriptures the things concerning himself."**[21]

---

[20] When we read that God spoke in many different ways in the past but in these days "through his Son" (Hebrews 1:1) the writer isn't implying that the message was new – just the way of delivering it. In the past the message was *about* his coming. In Jesus, the message *was* his coming. The truth was suddenly there in person.

[21] Luke 24:27.

So when the writer of Hebrews seems to speak disparagingly of "the Law" (the old covenant encoded at Sinai) as a failed system that never made anyone righteous,[22] it is important to realize that

a) True believers never relied on the Law of Moses for salvation, but always only on the grace of God.

b) The Old Testament code of Law was never intended by God to be a substitute or alternative way of attaining righteousness.

There were always true believers in Israel, as among its ancient ancestors. We easily remember a few prominent ones like Daniel, or Jeremiah. Such believers had no problem in walking righteously and using the Law as a guide for grace. But there were always thousands of others (as God reminded Elijah).[23]

The Law was only "weak" and "useless" for those who tried to make it a stand-alone source of righteousness and reward. It was only intended by God to give expression and direction to the righteousness of faith.

---

[22] *On the one hand a former commandment is set aside because of its weakness and uselessness (for the law made nothing perfect); on the other hand, a better hope is introduced, through which we draw near to God.* Hebrews 7:18-19.

[23] I Kings 19:18.

In itself the Law was good (Rom. 7:12) – but in its effectiveness it was flawed (Heb. 8:7) because of the hardness of so many of the people so much of the time (Heb. 8:9).

In the early days, Israel broke the Sinaitic covenant when they neglected their relationship with its giver. Wholesale idolatry was the result. But after the Babylonian exile, the Israelites increasingly fell into a different trap of using the Law to work up a sort of self-righteousness. They gravitated more and more to a spiritless legalism which had little to do with a relationship with God.

In the end God saw that it was best if the whole legal code was abolished – especially at a critical time when he intended to spread the Good News to the nations beyond Israel's borders in a way it had never been before.

So since the time of the Apostles, a new expression of the "covenant" has been preached worldwide, with no focus on codified law at all. Circumcision, and with it the whole ceremonial law, was abolished. So too, inevitably, was Israel's theocratic, national justice system.

But the "better hope" through Jesus, which the Hebrews writer emphasizes, was available all along for people of faith – even under the old covenant.[24] He contrasts only the new

---

[24] *The so-called dispensation of the law is replete with glorious promises...* Louis Berkhof, Systematic Theology, p 291.

expression of Good News in Christ with the misapplication of the Law by so many Israelites over the centuries.

And we must always remember Jesus' profound words: that he came to fulfil the Law, not to abolish it.[25] When we as his followers walk in love, the Law is written on our hearts – as God always meant it to be.

To argue that the Old Testament programme was never meant by God to be a source of spiritual life and blessing to the Israelites is to do him a great dishonour! Are we really to believe that it was all a divine hoax? Are we to imagine that he was only able to save a handful of people, now and then, just the famous men and women of faith whose names we know so well, but not the thousands of "ordinary" people? To believe so is to gravely belittle him.

---

[25] ... *and the so-called dispensation of grace did not abrogate the law as a rule of life* (Ibid, p 291). Cf. 1 Corinthians 7:19: *For neither circumcision nor uncircumcision counts for anything, but keeping the commandments of God.*

Strange things...

(3). The Spirit of God was *on* Old Testament believers but not *in* them

We must be clear that all true believers under the Old Testament received the same blessings as believers now in the New Testament dispensation.

In Romans 4, Paul emphasizes that Abraham received the gift of righteousness by faith (as we do) – and with it, the promised inheritance of the world: firstly the land of Israel, then the heavenly world to come. In Galatians 3, Paul teaches the same things (3:6-13), and summarizes this "blessing of Abraham" as receiving "the promise of the Spirit, through faith".

Louis Berkhof puts it emphatically:

> **"... these chapters teach that Abraham received in the covenant justification, including the forgiveness of sins and adoption into the very family of God, and also the gifts of the Spirit unto sanctification and eternal glory."**

When the writer of Hebrews talk of Old Testament saints dying without receiving what was promised, only seeing it "afar off" – he is not talking about their redemption but about their heavenly rewards at the resurrection.[26]

How has it come about that some Bible teachers can glibly say that Old Testament believers could only have had the blessing of the Spirit of God *on* them, but not *in* them?

There are two main reasons, as far as I can see:

i) An over-emphasis among Evangelicals on the importance of "legal" status before God – as opposed to actual, spiritual transformation. This allows a distorted view of God's saving plan whereby forgiveness of sins is seen as the basis of salvation, not spiritual regeneration.

ii) A misreading of verses in the Gospels and in Acts which seem to suggest the Holy Spirit could only have been given after Jesus' death, resurrection and ascension.

i) Legal Status versus Character Transformation

When Evangelicals emphasize the importance of man's

---

[26] Wayne Grudem is a little confused on this issue in his Systematic Theology (1994), p 117. He rightly talks of Old Testament believers being saved by a forward-looking faith (i.e. forward to Messiah) but then mistakenly uses Hebrews 11:13 to reference this. What they see "afar" in that verse is not their justification but its rewards (life in the heavenly country).

sinful record being cleared through the death of Jesus, there is a danger that we build our Christian faith on a negative foundation, even if the message overall is held to be a positive one. It allows people to think that a stain-free legal standing is enough to guarantee God's blessing – without Spiritual transformation. Is this therefore all the Old Testament saints had?

This view is untenable.

Let's think of an analogy. If you need a minimum bank account balance of €1 million to be eligible to live in the lovely Principality of Monaco, but in fact you are in debt and owe €50,000 – it won't help you get residency if someone is only willing to clear your €50,000 debt. Being debt-free won't get you a place in Monaco. They only want millionaires.

For Monaco substitute Heaven....[27]

Sometimes I worry that if you ask Evangelicals this question, "Is it enough to guarantee me a place in Heaven that Jesus 'paid' for my guilt on the Cross?" – in their unguarded moments, the natural instinct of many churchgoers might be to say *yes*.

---

[27] Reformed theologians then come up with quasi-Scholastic distinctions between Christ's *passive* obedience and his *active* obedience, both of which are somehow credited to our "account" – but still only by a vague *association*, not by a new life.

But what then of Paul's categorical statement?

> **"If anyone does not have the Spirit of Christ, he does not belong to him."**[28]

Or what of Jesus' emphatic utterance that "no one can enter the Kingdom of God unless he is born of the Spirit from above?"[29]

Oh yes, might come the afterthought: *justification leads to God's gift of the Spirit… and then all the rest.*

It almost seems like we have two gospels – or at least two bits of a gospel that really don't fit together very convincingly.

Reformed theologians, in an attempt to answer such questions begged by an insistence on a purely forensic[30] "justification" (so understood) have devoted much time to voluminous, convoluted theories as to how these central doctrines hang together.

---

[28] Romans 8:9.

[29] *Scripture does not leave us in doubt about the necessity of regeneration, but asserts this in the clearest terms. Jesus says: "Verily, verily, I say unto thee, Except a man be born again he cannot see the kingdom of God," John 3:3. This statement of the Saviour is absolute and leaves no room for exceptions.* Berkhof (ibid) p 472.

[30] "Forensic" means that it is an external, legal verdict by God as judge, rather than a spiritual transformation that takes place in us.

As I read their attempts, I am reminded for all the world of the medieval Scholastics – over-thinking things that should fit together intuitively, simply and beautifully.

But before going any further down that path, let me just ask a simple question about our Old Testament saints.

> *Who among our fellow Evangelicals will step forward and say that because they have New Testament blessings, they are categorically more spiritual than say a Daniel, or an Enoch, or the prophet Samuel?*

And if we admit (as seems obvious) that these were great spiritual men, how was that possible?[31] Were they children of God? Were they in God's family? Who would deny it? If so, how could they be, except by adoption through spiritual rebirth (Galatians 4:5-7)?

The whole theory of Old Testament believers living godly lives without the Holy Spirit of Christ inside them is indefensible.

But then if our theologians are determined to fit pieces

---

[31] *Man is described as dead through trespasses and sin, Ephesians 2:1, and this condition calls for nothing less than a restoration to life. A radical change is necessary... Scripture does not leave us in doubt about the necessity of regeneration.* Berkhof (ibid) p 472.

together that don't fit, and they seek to propose some strange mechanism by which Old Testament saints are somehow spiritualized after death – having been "justified" in life – are we really going to end up believing that people can be essentially changed after they die? That goes against the clear thrust of all the rest of scripture. Our bodies will be changed, yes – but the spiritual realities will be those that are already in place. They are to be "revealed" as Paul, Peter and John tell us in their Apostolic letters.

All mainstream Reformed theologians from Calvin and John Owen to Berkhof and Wayne Grudem agree that a new birth through the Spirit of Christ was the salvation of all believers in the Old Testament period.[32]

The problem remains, that if those early believers were in fact spirit-filled, how do we understand verses in scripture which say that the Holy Spirit would be "given" after Jesus returned to heaven? How could saints have received the Holy Spirit before then?

---

[32] Care needs to be taken however when we find Owen talking of "a larger" outpouring of the Spirit in the modern age. (Pneumatologia, or A Discourse Concerning the Holy Spirit, Book ii (1674) published online by Grand Rapids, Mi: Christian Classics Ethereal Library, p 148.) If he means numbers - agreed. But Grudem surely is a mile off target when he asserts that there was a "less powerful work of the Holy Spirit in individuals' lives during the old covenant" (Systematic Theology, p 771). That is untenable. Think of Samuel, Elijah or Daniel, to mention a few. And if God could give spiritual life to leaders, why on earth not to the rank and file?

ii) The Holy Spirit Given After Jesus' Ascension?

There are verses in the New Testament which seem to suggest that the coming of the Holy Spirit was a new phenomenon for an age ushered in by Jesus' resurrection and ascension to heaven.

To help us understand these texts properly, it is important to understand the background to the Pentecostal experience of Acts 2 and similar spiritual outpourings later in Acts. Then we can grasp more accurately what was "new" and what wasn't.

The most important aspect of the background is this. The big problem God had to deal with was that the outgoing covenant of Israel had acquired an unhelpful focus in the people's minds – an emphasis on the letter of the Law, not on its (God's) spirit. The whole programme was therefore generally failing.

In God's plans it was time for a new start. It was time to begin a new era, with a revised expression of the ancient covenant – one where the Spirit was more obviously at the centre of things. It must now be crystal clear that the promised blessing to Abraham and his descendants (the life-giving Spirit: cf. Galatians 3:2, and 14) would be offered as a free gift to believers purely on the grounds of their faith, and not because of observing the Law.

This was doubly important at that critical time in history when it was in God's mind and heart to spread the gospel beyond Israel's borders into the whole world. There must be no risk of confusion for Gentiles about how God's righteousness and its rewards were to be obtained.

This is why Paul fought so vehemently against Jews who reverted to circumcision and tried to foist it on Gentile believers. This must be a new era with unequivocal new arrangements.[33]

God the Father now granted Jesus the authority to pour out his Spirit in an unprecedented worldwide way. This was the Father's gift to Jesus (Acts 1:33) – and the tongues and prophesying were outward signs of this outpouring of spiritual blessing to all. This was to be the era of the Spirit – not of the Law (on its own). That was the key message. And to make the spiritual heart of the gospel clear to everyone, the Spirit would be "given" to believers in a special, very public and visible way – with miraculous signs of "tongues" and inspired prophetic praise.

---

[33] ... even though, as Paul taught, the righteousness of faith was always God's only intended way of salvation. The Law had never been offered as an alternative means of salvation (Galatians 3:17-18).

This is the background we must grasp when we come to look at Acts 2. According to Joel's prophecy quoted by Peter, this was a special day marked by spiritual manifestations. It was, in modern terms, a revival.

Against this backcloth, Peter was able to preach the Good News in a clear, simple, and "new" way, without reference to the Law or other complications:

> **"Repent and be baptized every one of you in the name of Jesus Christ for the forgiveness of sins; and you shall receive the gift of the Holy Spirit. For the promise is to you and your children, and to all that are far off, everyone whom the Lord our God calls to him."**[34]

Incidentally, some preachers make much of Peter's boldness on this day, contrasting it to the apparent fearfulness of the Apostles beforehand. It is thought the disciples had been cowering in some "upper room" (Acts 1:13). But the last verse in Luke's gospel states that the disciples "were continually in the Temple blessing God". And when Peter got up to speak about electing a new Apostle (Acts 1:15) we are told there were 120 people in his audience. This was not a small group of timid believers huddling in a dark attic! At Pentecost, he had an audience of 3,000 people present.

---

[34] Acts 2:38.

So Pentecost was the fanfare start of a new era. The signs attested that:

"He has poured out this which you see and hear."

But we shouldn't think for a moment that Peter and the other Apostles received the Spirit for the first time on that day of Pentecost. Or that all other believers before then had no deep experience of the Holy Spirit.

Peter himself had already shown the supernatural insight of a man whose spirit had been renewed when he had confessed Jesus as the son of God (Matthew 6:16). Consider that in the light of Paul's words: "The unspiritual man cannot grasp the things of the Spirit of God for they are foolishness to him." Or again, "No one can say Jesus is Lord except by the Spirit of God" (1 Corinthians 12:3).

Nor were Peter and the others only regenerated in that late episode recorded in John 20:22 when we read that Jesus "breathed on them" and said "receive the Holy Spirit". That benediction was connected with power for ministering the gospel (John 20:23; cf. Luke 10:5 and Luke 24:47) – the power Jesus promised would come in a special way as they waited for it in Jerusalem.[35] He

---

[35] *When Jesus breathed on his disciples and said to them "Receive the Holy Spirit" (John 20:22), it probably was an acted out prophecy of what would happen to them at Pentecost.* Grudem (ibid) p 769.

wasn't giving disciples new life in the Spirit for the first time – just predicting a powerful continuation of their (and his) ministry.

Pentecost was a baptism of power for uniquely successful ministry by the disciples, with special public signs to mark the beginning of a dispensation that would change nations. The spectacular event accomplished God's primary aim of putting the Spirit centre-stage for a new drama that would soon be broadcast worldwide.

But it did not mark the disciples' spiritual rebirth. It did for the many new converts on that momentous day.

In later developments in Acts, God continued to put the same spotlight on the miraculous, spiritual nature of the new gospel when subsequent converts also received the free gift and showed the same signs.

Where this outward-focused "anointing" coincided with the new birth of converts, there is no doctrinal confusion. The Spirit of regeneration within them was the Spirit of power that could be seen and heard in the external signs.

Problems arise because in some episodes in Acts there seems to be a two-phase experience of salvation. Some churches maintain that this should be viewed as the normal Christian experience.

If we remember God's primary intention in this new dispensation – of placing a public spotlight on the freely given Spirit – we will more easily understand what was going on in those developments, why there sometimes seemed to be a delay between people's conversion and the conferring of outward signs of spiritual life.

However it is worth mentioning in passing that in the case of the Ephesian "disciples" in Acts 9, it is possible they may not have had true faith until Paul spoke to them. They might have been among the crowds who simply followed John the Baptist into the Jordan looking for a new age for oppressed Israel, without a personal saving knowledge of the gospel. It's even possible they had not been in Israel themselves but had been baptized second-hand by people who had.[36]

In other cases it was almost certainly only the outward signs of a particular anointing of an already present Spirit which was the result of the Apostles laying on hands. It was critically important for God to show publicly that the gospel reaching Samaria and beyond was part of the same spiritual wave that had been received in Jerusalem.

---

[36] The literal translation of Paul's question is: "Did you receive the Holy Spirit believing?" He seemed to be asking simply, "Did you believe and receive the Holy Spirit?" Acts19:2.

The gift of the Spirit comes to believers at conversion as the seal of God's promises. It may or may not come with exactly the same signs as in those early days of the Apostles. But it is the same blessing. It is a unique, unrepeatable and complete experience for believers. It gives us all we need for life and godliness.

Some people seem to experience a sudden new lease of life and power at a later stage in their Christian journey.[37] But this cannot be the basis for a doctrine of a two-stage salvation, with conversion being followed by a separate "baptism in the Spirit."

> " ... no one is questioning that Christians can have a second experience of God's grace, or a third one, or a fourth.... Many who hold that might call it a "new consecration" or something like that.... But sometimes it is much more than a quibble about words because fundamental Christian doctrine is involved, and people are led astray and confused... Conversion and the new birth, and the baptism of the Spirit are all to do with the one thing. It is the coming of God, the coming of Jesus, the coming of the Holy Spirit to your life... Is there progress? Are there subsequent experiences? Oh yes! But whatever names you use, do not try to say

---

[37] Paul, Peter and Steven are recorded as having special "baptisms", infillings or anointings of the Holy Spirit for particular challenges at different moments in Acts: 4:8; 7:55; 13:9. These instances put the "baptism" of the disciples at Pentecost in perspective and align all such experiences with similar instances recorded in the Old Testament.

> that God has half-come and that he is going to whole-come next time... God is one, and God coming into my heart is one."[38]

The outward signs of spiritual *baptism* in those early days of the church were the fanfare of a new covenant – a new age of spiritual blessing. The Spirit of God, poured out through Jesus, would be the inspiration of this new church, their comforter, their ongoing strength and teacher, in a thousand ways that even Jesus, limited to one body in one place, could not have been. In that sense, it was "better" that he should "go to the Father" and pour out these spiritual blessings. With the Father's authority he launched a new era of spiritual revival and power.

It was not a new gospel – it was an old one, a very old one – proclaimed now afresh to the world in the clearest terms, without reference to the Law of Sinai, and backed by spiritual signs.

But always in Israel's history, clustered in untold numbers around God's covenant of grace, were the hosts of believing men and women of faith, like Simeon or Anna (Luke 2:25-38) – devout, steadfast, and full of the Spirit – waiting to join the ranks of the heroes of faith and enter triumphantly, with us, into Heaven's glories through the Messiah.

---

[38] William Still, Theological Studies (1990), pp 169-174.

Meditations

Why does God not appear more often?

Consider the Flowers in the Field

Wouldn't it be nice?...

Meditations

Why does God not appear more often?

I'm sure most Christians have asked themselves this question at some stage in their lives. Why does the Lord not appear to us more regularly, in visible, physical form? It would be so easy for him to do. Or maybe just let us see an angel? It would mean so much to us, wouldn't it? Just once....

Peter the Apostle encourages us with the assurance that those who love God without seeing Him will inherit a special blessing: "Without having seen him, you love him; though you do not now see him you believe in him and rejoice with unutterable and exalted joy. As the outcome of your faith you obtain the salvation of your souls." Paul takes up the same theme in 2 Cor.4:16-18.

God is training our faith – to live daily lives guided by what we can't see, including the promised future blessings. This faith is what pleases God (Hebrews 11:6).

Every time we make decisions based on the invisible truths of the Kingdom, God is working a deep spiritual magic in us – undoing the damage we inherited from Adam's sin.

Eve and Adam did see the Lord. But they stopped

believing he is who he says he is; that he (alone) is the source of blessing; that rejecting him and his word means death.

So we have been called to live in a dispensation of faith, not sight.

Having established this order, God does not usually like to work against his own economy. Every day's training in faith is a spiritual workout by which God is preparing us radically for Heaven. And as we embrace it, as C. S. Lewis puts it, we "tread Adam's dance backwards".

A couple that has enjoyed a romantic courtship but lived apart prior to their wedding day will know what a special day that will be, as they begin a new life together. And for Christian believers, what a glorious prospect lies ahead of us – to one day see our Creator, our Lover, face to face. We will nearly burst with joy!

Then we will "know in fullness, even as we have been fully known".

Meditations

Consider the Flowers in the Field...

When Jesus encouraged us to look at nature to see God's providence in action, he pointed us towards a lifestyle where we can relax about our tomorrows. God provides. That was his message. If the Father has built productive principles into nature, so that even plants and wild birds flourish within pre-ordained processes, how much more will this be the case for us?

Jesus' teaching is about getting into the flow of God's purposes. The example of the beautiful flowers gives us some simple but profound lessons.

Different Phases
In nature, different phases follow each other according to God's design. Very few flowers are radiant all the time. Months hidden under ground may be followed by slow, non-spectacular growth, before summer comes with its magnificent blossoms. But all the processes are necessary to get to that spectacular flowering.

Enjoy the Waiting
You can't rush God's timing. It's always perfect – and is worth waiting for, even if we easily feel

frustrated. Thankfully, God gives us plenty to appreciate in the present, otherwise waiting for the future could seem intolerable. Enjoy the wait, in fellowship with him! There are blessings to relish every day. And you'll enjoy the future blessings all the more when they come.

Natural and Supernatural
God's ways in our lives can often seem so natural that it takes faith to realize he is at work at all! God likes working within natural processes (including time), for he made them. Only rarely and for special reasons does he intervene in "supernatural" ways. When he does, we have an obvious miracle. But God is always at work – and his power is no less miraculous when one thing seems naturally to lead to another in our lives. The magic is hidden. We sometimes just need to take a step back to see these miracles.

So let's relax. If we believe we are in God's will, we can go with the flow – his flow – and see where it takes us. He has it all under control, and unless we deliberately step outside his purposes, we can't go wrong.

"The path of the righteous is like the light of dawn that shines brighter and brighter unto full day."[39]

---

[39] Proverbs 4:18.

Meditations

Wouldn't it be nice?...

Don't we wish sometimes that life were simpler? If only things could be more clear-cut... what to do, where to go, and when. We pray for guidance about a new job, or moving house, and then we sometimes seem to be left to find our own way. Wouldn't it be nice some morning to wake up to a precise list of instructions, along with our bowl of Cornflakes!?

The reason?

God is treating us like Royalty.

We were made in his image; crowned princes and princesses; lords of creation. That is our dignity. He will not dictate to us what to do every step of the way – any more than a good parent would dream of telling grown-up children what to eat or what to wear every day.

Free will is the heart of the amazing autonomy God wants for us. He intends us to live our lives with dignity within the earthly frameworks he has given us – not operating like robots. If things are in danger of going wrong, he has gentle ways of nudging us in the right direction, closing doors here, opening some there; but never so as to undermine our autonomy.

This is the paradox of the Christian life. God is closer to us than any human relative, and yet he gives us more space and liberty than even the best of human parents do. We pray for a lifestyle where our will is his will (the model Jesus set); we want to live in him, with him, for him, inspired by him: as Paul says in Colossians 3:17, "Whatever you do in word or deed, do everything in the name of the Lord Jesus." But we never stop being free, self-determining human beings. Not even for a day.

Sometimes God does intervene with firm, detailed directives at critical times in the life of a nation, the church or individuals. But always within limits.

So the next time we seem to get a frustrating silence from our Heavenly Father, let's believe that he is simply trusting us to get up and "get on with it".

And then, years later, when we look back over our lives' many paths, we will see how everything ultimately fitted into his wonderful plans. And we'll be thankful.

PART 2

CHILDREN OF THE LIVING GOD

Children Of The Living God

If you want to judge how well a person understands Christianity, find out how much he makes of the thought of being God's child, and having God as his father.[40]

* * * * * * * * * *

What a piece of work is a man, how noble in reason, how infinite in faculties, in form and moving how express and admirable, in action how like an angel, in apprehension how like a god![41]

* * * * * * * * * *

How wonderful is God's creation of Man! We have been made in his image. What a privilege. What amazing dignity we were born to share. We should never stop thinking about that.

Biblically, this means more than just being made to resemble him. Being in someone's image, in the scriptures, is evidence of sonship. In Genesis 5:3, we read how Adam became the father of Seth "in his own likeness, after his image".

---

[40] J.I. Packer (1973) Knowing God. London: Hodder and Stoughton. Cited in "Children of the Living God", Sinclair Ferguson (1989).

[41] William Shakespeare. Hamlet, Act 2, Scene 2.

The writer of Hebrews takes up this sonship theme when he emphasizes that Jesus Christ "reflects" God's glory (like an image) and "bears the very stamp of his nature". Paul likewise declares that "he (Jesus) is the image of the invisible God, the first born of all creation."

It is amazing that what the scriptures proclaim so gloriously about Christ, was written also about Man in the beginning. We were made in God's glorious image. We were his children.

Tragically, this likeness of God in us was lost through Adam's fall. Paul writes how we have all "fallen short of the glory of God"[42] through sinfulness. Man lost the glory of his Father which he reflected.

Then the gospel of Jesus bursts victoriously into mankind's history, with redemptive power, to undo the damage;[43] to restore us to our destiny – of being children, heirs of God the Creator himself.

What a great honour is ours – to be adopted as children of God. Not by a legal transaction in an account book somewhere, but by the miracle of new birth from above.

---

[42] Romans 3:23.

[43] *The reason the son of God appeared was to destroy the works of the devil.* 1 John 3:8.

Some people might even be shocked how boldly Peter describes our redeemed humanity:

> "We have become partakers of the divine nature."[44]

The New Testament scriptures are full of this wonderful truth.

> "You have received the spirit of *sonship*."[45]

> "Beholding the glory of God we are being changed *into his likeness*, from one degree of glory to another."[46]

This process of re-glorification in our Father's image has begun. It will end in an unimaginable explosion of perfection when we see him face to face.

> "Beloved we are God's children now. It does not yet appear what we shall be, but we know that when he appears we shall be like him for we shall see him as he is."[47]

---

[44] 2 Peter 1:4.

[45] Romans 8:15-16.

[46] 2 Corinthians 3:18.

[47] 1 John 3:2. Cf. "The creation waits with eager longing for the revealing of the sons of God" (Romans 8:19).

What the first Adam lost for us by disobedience, Christ, the second Adam, has regained for us through his perfect obedience. We are back in God's family.

> **"See what love the father has given to us, that we should be called the children of God; and so indeed we are."**[48]

* * * * * * * * * * * * * *

If all this is true, what are the things that hinder us from walking with heads held high as Christian princes and princesses? Why are we not always overflowing with joy, confidence, and grateful excitement?

To use a common English idiom: why are we so often "down on ourselves"?

In the next section I am going to try to shed light on three common areas of confusion which may make us lose sight of our heavenly dignity and calling.

---

[48] 1 John 3:1.

Why Are We So Often Down On Ourselves?

(1) Wrong perspectives on man's place in the universe

(2) Exaggerating the difference between God and man

(3) An over-emphasis on being "sinners"

Down on ourselves?...

(1) Wrong perspectives on man's place in the universe

When the Psalmist looked up at the skies, he was tempted for a moment to be over-awed and to focus on our paltry size.

> *"When I consider the works of thy hands, the sun and the moon which thou hast ordained, what is man that thou art mindful of him, or the son of man that thou considerest him?"*[49]

How small and frail we are compared to the great cosmos around us.

But he didn't stop there.

Many Christians do….

Rather, the Psalmist had an inspired revelation of the dignity of man as the crown of creation – God' own sons and daughters. He had a vision of Christ, and (the new) mankind embodied, epitomized in him.

---

[49] Psalm 8:3-4.

For us too, instead of being over-awed by what scientists tell us about the vastness of the cosmos, we should feel all the more special! To think that God has made all this for us, his heirs! It is all ours.[50] Each human life means infinitely more to our Father God than a billion galaxies. We must never forget that. We mustn't doubt it – not for a minute.

Every amazing scientific discovery should glorify God and help deepen our relationship with him. It should cause us to praise him – for two reasons: firstly the wonder of the phenomenon itself (e.g. the stupendous size of the universe); secondly, the ingenuity of men and women who uncover and chart these astonishing truths about God's creation.

There should never be any opposition between true science and religion. The real problem has always been man's deep-rooted refusal to acknowledge God as God. Today it can be dressed up in more sophisticated scientific theories, but it has always been the same root rejection of the Creator.

We can give the last word on this to Calvin:

> ***"Can anything be more detestable than this madness in man, who, finding God a hundred times both in his body and his soul, make his excellence in this respect a***

---

[50] 1 Corinthians 3:22.

pretext for denying that there is a God?"[51]

"For no sooner do we, from a survey of the world, obtain some slight knowledge of Deity, than we pass by the true God, and set up in his stead the dream and phantom of our own brain, drawing away the praise of justice, wisdom and goodness from the fountain-head, and transferring it to some other quarter."[52]

The sad irony is that when men and women fail to see God as Creator, they lose sight of their own dignity. They reduce themselves to insignificant specks of breathing matter in a vast, meaningless cosmos, whereas we were always destined to be children of the living God.

---

[51] Institutes, Vol 1 p 53.

[52] Ibid pp 62-63.

Down on ourselves?...

(2) Exaggerating the difference between God and man

There is a popular song used in recent years in modern churches that contains the following line:

" *No eye has seen, no ear has heard…*"[53]

People use this to talk about God's heavenly purposes. We love the poetry of that thought…. We enjoy the sense of holy mystery that it brings.

Unfortunately it is a total misquotation – nice-sounding words taken badly of context.

What Paul goes on to say at that point in his letter is that God has revealed these previous mysteries to us. They are not unknown any more. Each believer has the Spirit of God, who searches the very depths of God, and reveals them to

---

[53] *How Great is Your Love*, by Mark Altrogge. The quotation is used in a similarly careless way in many online blogs or Websites, e.g.
http://biblestudyplanet.com/what-heaven-will-be-like/

us, says Paul.[54]

Elsewhere he states this truth in similar bold terms:

" We have the mind of Christ."

This may sit uncomfortably with those who have an exaggerated view of the distance between God and man. Self-deprecating thoughts may seem to be a humble, holy response to the greatness of God. But God made us in his image. We are children in his family. Why would we not expect him to reveal his mysteries to us?

It is true, there are some things we will only properly understand when we get to heaven's vantage point. But for now, I think there is a danger of setting our sights too low, doing ourselves down and giving up too soon in our desire to understand the deepest mysteries of God.

Another passage that is similarly misquoted is, "My thoughts are not your thoughts, nor are your ways my ways, says the Lord" (Isaiah 55:8). Again this seems to put a holy distance between us and God. But again it is badly quoted out of context.

God was appealing to an apostate people who needed to repent and change their ways. He is not describing the

---

[54] 1 Corinthians 2:9-10

normal Man-God relationship.

On the contrary, God expects us to walk so closely to him that we can say the things we hear him saying, and work with him in what we see him doing. Being on the same wavelength as God is the normal Christian life, says the Apostle John:

> **"... whoever says he abides in him ought to walk in the same way in which he walked."[55]**

So let's do ourselves a huge favour and stop indulging in false modesty about our position before God! Self-abasement may seem to be giving God his place – but it is not proper humility. And it will seriously damage our spiritual life.

If we want to see how close Man can be to God, we only need to think of the fact that the eternal Son of God became a man and lived for 33 years in a humble earthly context in a Roman province.

What does that tell us about our human life in this world, and our closeness to deity? Such an amazing joining of God and Man was only possible because in the beginning God had made Man with his own family image.

That image has been restored in us. We are children of God. That is the heart of the gospel.

---

[55] I John 2:6.

Down on ourselves?...

(3) An over-emphasis on being "sinners"

The distorted humility described above can also be due to our awareness of human imperfection. We know we have really fallen short of the mark. We have messed things up, over and over again. We've been guilty of many mistakes and deficiencies. In fact Paul says starkly, that "in me there dwells no good thing."

BUT...

We have been given a new life – nothing less than the life of Christ in us. The old sinful "us" is dead and gone. It died with him on the Cross.

"It is no longer I who live but Christ who lives in me."[56]

We live the new life of the Spirit, which helps us to be properly human again, with all our redeemed individuality. Dying to sin and the world with Christ doesn't make us any less ourselves, or any less human. Through him we become properly human. We discover who we were really meant to be and experience the richness of life as God intended. We

---

[56] Galatians 2:20.

won't reach perfection until we enter heaven – but we are being changed every day now "from glory to glory", as we "walk in the Spirit".

It sounds very pious in certain churches when members recite the following words from their liturgy and call themselves "miserable offenders":

> *"Almighty and most merciful Father;*
> *We have erred, and strayed from Thy ways like lost sheep.*
> *We have followed too much the devices and desires of our own hearts.*
> *We have offended against Thy holy laws.*
> *We have left undone those things which we ought to have done;*
> *And we have done those things which we ought not to have done;*
> *And there is no health in us."*

But it's not Biblical.

It is true that "in me there dwells no good thing". But equally, *"it is no longer I who live but Christ who lives in me"*. We don't stop being Jill Bradley or Peter McDonald, with all our differences in temperament and abilities, but we have a new Christian identity. We have become *"partakers of the divine nature"*. It really dishonours God's handiwork in us if we insist on saying "there is no health in us".

HE is in us!

Every Sunday, in less liturgical churches as well, there is the regular, scheduled confession of all the things we've done or not done during the week since the last Lord's Day service.

This seems so different from what we are told in Hebrews is the normal Christian experience:

> "... the worshippers, cleansed once for all, would no longer have any consciousness of sin."[57]

Commenting on a mindset where Christians don't feel they are humble enough unless they are constantly lamenting their failings, C. S. Lewis simply pointed out, "It doesn't sound much like love, joy and peace in the Holy Spirit to me!"

Why do some Christians experience so little of this joyful, spirit-filled life?

Could it be that our continual obsession with our sinfulness is a sort of self-fulfilling prophecy? The more we focus on being "sinners", the more guilty and weak we feel. In fact, we are allowing ourselves to slip back under the Law, wrongly applied. If not ultimately "falling away from grace", we are certainly undermining its transforming power in our lives.

If we do slip up in some way, we ought to say, with Paul, that it is not I who have sinned (because "I" have been crucified) but it is sin. It is the residue of an old life. It is only a depersonalized force – not a sinful identity. It wasn't me!

---

[57] Hebrews 10:2.

The new me is righteous. And I am not a split personality.

How could Christ be other than righteous? He is my new identity; his spirit joining with my spirit to create a new person; still recognizable as me, but now a son or daughter of the Most High.

That should make us walk with heads held high. The devil will accuse us. Our thoughts can often accuse us. Others from time to time will want to accuse us. But from God there is no condemnation. We have been made righteous, once and for all, with his own life. Sin is a past issue. We can shrug it off, like Lazarus coming out of the tomb, leaving behind the clothes that belonged to the grave.

Dr Rainer Hauke, in his daring book about the German Reformer Andreas Osiander, points out that for too long, when we have talked in church about being "justified sinners", the emphasis has been loudly on the word *sinners*, and much more quietly on being made *righteous*. He goes on to quote Ingmar Bergman as saying that Protestantism offers not so much forgiveness as a lifelong mountain of guilt.[58]

People who find it hard to distance themselves from a sinful identity will argue using verses in John's first letter, where the Apostle writes, "If we say we have no sin, we

---

[58] *Als evangelischer Christ habe ich zu sagen: ich bin Sünder; zwar bin ich ein gerechtfertigter Sünder, aber das "gerechtfertigt" klingt leise – Sündersein, das kommt mit Wucht: Für Ingmar Bergman "kennt der Protestantismus keinerlei Vergebung, nur ein lebenslang wachsendes Schuldgebirge."* Dr Rainer Hauke, Gott-Haben – um Gottes Willen (1999) Frankfurt am Main: Peter Lang GmbH.

deceive ourselves."

But this is taken out of context. John was writing against emerging heresies at the time, including Dualism and an early form of Gnosticism, with distorted views of existence and the way of salvation. He is not advocating confession as a perpetual, chest-beating way of life. He is pointing to the universal nature of sin in the fallen human condition.

Clutching on to our sinfulness is not the way of the Christian. On the contrary, the whole thrust of that letter from John affirms a new, sin-free lifestyle that Christians should expect to enjoy (1 John 3:4-6; 5:2). He is very positive about this.

Again, people might quote the example Jesus gave when he described the tax collector "beating his breast" and begging for forgiveness in the Temple. But this was to show two different approaches to gaining God's mercy generally in our lives. Jesus is talking about life choices based either on faith or on self. He is not advocating regular self-flagellation.

If we find that we need to retrain our thinking after years of dim views of ourselves, it might help gain a healthy psychological distance from sin if we stopped praying for forgiveness! That may sound shocking. But God has already forgiven us, once and for all.[59] He chose not to hold our sins

---

[59] *What are you more conscious of today? Your sins or the fact that you have been forgiven? My friend, don't be conscious of your sins. Be conscious instead of Jesus and His finished work. The Lamb of God **has** taken away **all** your sins at the cross, so count on the fact that you are a forgiven child of God!* Joseph Prince: http://www.josephprince.org/daily-grace/grace-inspirations/single/count-on-

against us when he decided to give us new life and membership in his family. That can't be altered. We can't add to it or take away from it. It's done and it is irrevocable.

Of course, we can make a mess of our lives in this world if we go too far back down paths of wrong behaviour. But then it is the temporal consequences we have to face, not eternal condemnation. Many of the passages such as those in Hebrews that talk about falling away and its consequences are referring to the aftermath of persistent sin in this life (only). Our standing before God, our eternal destiny and our identity, once we are saved, are never in doubt.

If we do slip up and sin gets the better of us, of course we want the Lord to know we are sorry. We want to regain full enjoyment of fellowship with him as quickly as possible. We don't want anything in our "flesh" to stand between us.

But to help us realize that we don't need to ask again for (eternal) forgiveness, and so as not to identify ourselves again with the power of sin, perhaps "sorry" is all we need to say. Let's use a different word. We have already been forgiven, to the remarkable extent of being made a son or daughter.

We can't become any more righteous or acceptable by endless confessions. We can't change or lose our identity. "I am a new creation… It is no longer I who live, but Christ who lives in me."

---

gods-forgiveness/

If we fall, "It is no longer I who sin but sin that dwells in me."

My sinfulness has been dealt with. It is an utterly past issue, even if it can be a temporary annoyance.

Meditations

Sculpted to Perfection

The Family Business. Why is prayer so important?

The Painting

Meditations

Sculpted to Perfection

Michelangelo's statue of David in Florence – carved out of a single block of marble, 17 feet high – is a sublime masterpiece. It is a work of genius that takes your breath away, especially when you see it close up. The artist worked on it with passion for three years, often sleeping in his clothes so that he could start earlier in the morning on his labour of love.

This is the way God is working with us, turning his constant, skilful attention to us day by day, patiently creating the masterpieces he has in his mind's eye – each one of us different, but each one transformed ultimately into the image of Christ, who is perfection.

There must have been times in the early stages of Michelangelo's work when the artist needed to remove large chunks of marble in order to get the shape roughly right. But even more impressive, when you look at the end-product, are the many little subtleties of perfection that make the work mesmerizing.

Knowing that God, the Master Artist, wants to perfect us, we should be on the lookout for daily opportunities to cooperate with his design, as he labours to make us more like his Son. He is often chiseling spiritually with a fine tool to smooth a line here, or perfect a lovely feature there.

When someone else gets praise, or promotion, or an opportunity which we felt we deserved, let's smile and take it with good grace, seeing it as an opportunity to trust in God for our reward and glory that lasts. Let's see God's hand in the test and let the process have its effect on us, even if it is painful. It is shaping us.

And every time that we allow the Spirit to mould us deep inside like this, God brings us one bit closer to becoming the finished masterpieces that one day will take angels' breath away.

Meditations

The Family Business

Why is prayer so important?

This is a question we can't avoid asking. If God is all-powerful and always gets his way in the end, why should we bother praying? Why does God need us to pray to get things done?

I see it as our role in the family business. The Lord is giving us a chance to manage the world along with him. When we pray, we are bringing his power into situations to produce good results. We are co-creating with him.

As human beings we are made "in his likeness". Among other things this involves us being responsible, working and creating like him. It's our privilege to share in his work and be like him.

Does he really need us to pray? What if we didn't? Would things still get done?

Yes – I guess so. But we wouldn't enjoy the privilege of helping him with the important jobs. Others would be given the responsibility instead of us.

This doesn't mean we should feel under pressure to pray for anything and everything. We should direct our prayers to things which we really have faith for. In life generally each of us has different responsibilities; we are all called to different walks of life. Similarly we can assume that the Lord also wants us to be involved in different areas of creative prayer. We can't take it all on.

How can we tell what areas we really have faith for – as opposed to wishful thinking? To get involved creatively with God we must be able to see what *he* is doing – then accept our prayerful part in that work with him. This means staying in tune with him.

Faith is not just positive thinking which we can muster up at will if we just try hard enough. It is a product that grows naturally out of a close relationship with the Lord, where we understand his ways, appreciate his power, and see and hear what he is doing and saying. This is the way Jesus lived, with his eye always on the Father.

Closeness to God is the basis of faith.

People are sometimes rebuked in the Biblical records for not having faith. We might think that is hard. It's not their fault (you might think): either you believe something or you don't.

But Jesus sees unbelief as a mark of an immature relationship. So when he says that certain demons can only be driven out by prayer and fasting, he doesn't mean that we need to make more effort to get some magic formula right. He means we need to purify and deepen our walk with him, to be close enough to really see him at work and tap into *his* power. In praying, we have to stay focussed on the Lord – his person, his will and his work.

It's the family business to make things better.

Prayer is one of the ways we share that work with the Lord.

Meditations

The Painting

A famous artist of the last century had painted a masterpiece, one that he loved more than all the rest of his work. He was happy to sell any of his other paintings, but this one would never leave his house, he said. It had pride of place in his home, and it gave him enormous pleasure every day just to look at it.

The painter had to travel a lot on business. Upon his return home from one trip, he was greeted with the news that his most precious painting was in the hands of a local loan shark. His remorseful wife had organized a gambling party one evening… and things had got out of hand.

Heartbroken, the artist tried to buy back his work. But the mobster wanted a fortune to part with it. Tragically, the new owner didn't even appreciate art. The painting was flung into a damp cellar and lay there neglected and damaged.

The artist worked harder than ever to sell more paintings and save enough money to get his beloved masterpiece back. And eventually, the painting was returned to its rightful owner – at a high cost. He lovingly restored it, bit by bit. He gave it a new frame. Soon it hung again in its original place at the heart of his home.

And it was more precious to him than ever.

PART 3

DOUBLE TAKE

Being Made Righteous

It seems strange that while God was clearly intent on emphasizing the central place of the Holy Spirit in the newly proclaimed Good News two thousand years ago, we in western evangelicalism have traditionally put the main spotlight on another doctrine: "Justification", understood as the forgiveness of sins through a sacrificial *propitiation*.[60]

But what if we could see the two things, spiritual rebirth and "justification", as one and the same thing?

That is exactly what we find in Paul's statement to Titus:

> **"... he saved us ... by the Holy Spirit's washing of regeneration and renewal so that being justified by his grace we might become heirs of eternal life."**[61]

Spiritual rebirth gives us our "justification". The apparent tension between these two major gospel emphases over the years is dispelled with one stroke when we can simply understand "justified" to mean "made righteous" – not in a legal account book somewhere (as traditionally viewed); but in reality and experience, through regeneration in the Spirit.

---

[60] Appeasing an angry God.

[61] Titus 3:5-7.

On the basis of that understanding, we are not made righteous according to some system of credit, where we are *"regarded"* as righteous because of Christ, but we are made righteous by transformation, through the new life of Christ given to us in his Spirit.

Then our most important doctrines come together beautifully. The Greek word δικαιωθέντες (dikaiothentes), often translated "justified" means: ***made righteous.***[62] When we speak about "justification", we are talking about being renewed, being born "from above" by the Holy Spirit.

Although the word "justified" has a long and venerable history, it is actually a very unhelpful translation if we seek to trace connections within and across Paul's letters. We lose the important links to his use of the words "righteous" (δικαίους - dikaious) and "righteousness" (δικαιοσύνη - dikaiosune).

Δικαιωθέντες (dikaiothentes) is from the same Greek root; so why introduce a completely different sounding word (*justified* [63]) alongside "righteous" and "righteousness"? This enables an extra meaning to be slipped in – the so-called *forensic* view of "justification" as a transaction that takes place outside us and is based on a legal verdict.

---

[62] E.g. Romans 5:1 – *Therefore having been made righteous by faith, we have peace with God.*

[63] E.g. Titus 3:7 (NIV, ESV etc).

As a result of manipulating translated words like this, traditional interpretations are reinforced and perpetuated.

After years of accepting the external, forensic interpretation of "being justified" as *gospel truth*, I realize that this double take on something so fundamental can come as a great shock to many evangelicals.

But what we have received as "gospel" is actually an interpretation of this key concept, arrived at by the majority of the 16th century reformers.

Not by all of them....

Andreas Osiander, one of the great German Reformation leaders who worked effectively alongside Luther, held that *justification* meant "to be made righteous", in essence,[64] through God's own righteousness, implanted in us by his Holy Spirit.

His views created a furore! Lutherans and Calvinists united to insist on a forensic meaning of justification.

Among the many published objections arguing why Osiander was wrong in his view of justification, his opponents argued that there was not enough objective

---

[64] *Imparted* righteousness (in substance), not merely *imputed* (in a courtroom ledger).

assurance for believers in that inner-focused gospel.[65]

But in that line of argument, these opponents seemed to have confused the inner nature of righteousness with subjective uncertainty. It doesn't follow.

Why should it be easier to believe in an external declaration of righteousness than in an actual implanted righteousness? We may experience its power more or less within our lives; we may cultivate it more or less in practice: but we can still always believe that there is an "imperishable seed" within us.

In fact, we are expressly encouraged to see the Holy Spirit within us as a cast-iron guarantee of our eternal inheritance. We *can* be totally objective about it, and fully assured, even if it is internal. We are expected to be!

Another aspect which Osiander's opponents attacked in his teaching was that in emphasizing the importance of God's essential righteousness in our salvation, he seemed to undervalue the righteousness of Christ won by his obedience as a man.[66]

---

[65] Cf. Typical reactions outlined by Timothy Wengert, in Defending Faith, (2012): p 31 (Roting); p 49 (the Brandenburg-Küstrin theologians).

[66] Ibid p 35 (responses from Bugenhagen et al focusing on "Christological" problems); p 41 (ditto Amsdorf); p 42 (in the joint response from Vorpommern presented by Johann Knipstro). Cf. also Hauke (Gott-Haben, 1999) on recent Finnish Osiander research (p 66).

Perhaps Osiander did over-emphasize the divine nature of Christ's righteousness at the expense of his work as a man. Jesus became the new, second Adam, for our sakes. His divine righteousness can only be effective to save us because it was lived out as a human life. He had to live as a man, resisting sin to the end (even crucifixion) so that he could give us *his* victorious, righteous, and truly human life.

That is the main theme of the letter to the Hebrews. Jesus became, as it were, our High priest, by living a human life as our saving representative, our pioneer.

But if Osiander didn't emphasize enough the human outworking of Jesus' righteousness as a man (he didn't deny it), this doesn't detract from his radical understanding that spiritual transformation is the basis of our salvation, not a "legal fiction":

We are made righteous by God's implanted righteousness.

This is why Peter was able to say that we "have become partakers of the divine nature".

In the end, it seemed that the real reason most of the other Reformation leaders were jittery with the idea of implanted righteousness rather than an external *imputed* one, was that it smacked too much of Roman Catholicism. It was dangerously close to the Roman idea of "infusing" grace, with its emphasis on Christian character ("works") as proof of salvation and the basis of heavenly blessings to come.[67]

Had Osiander lived in another age, his central understanding of "justification" might have received a better theological hearing. But at a time when the Protestant church was trying to establish its doctrines over against centuries of Roman dominance, Osiander was considered dangerous.

Some said he was in the pay of the Pope.

Others that he was possessed by the devil.

---

[67] "...er (Melanchthon) und seine Schüler fürchteten jeden Seitenblick auf Gottes erneuerndes Handeln an uns im Zusammenhange der Rechtfertigungslehre als ein Katholisieren..." Paul Althaus (1920) cited in Hauke (Gott-Haben, 1999) p 55.

You Have Heard It Said...

(1) Forgiveness

(2) Declarative Righteousness

(3) Proof Texts and Fantasies

(4) "New" Perspectives on Paul

(5) "Justification" and "Sanctification"

(6) Romans 7 – The Controversial "Man"

You have heard it said…

(1). Forgiveness

God hates sin. There can be no doubt about that. He hates it with an eternal and profound hatred. It makes him rage. He will never allow it one quarter of an inch in his Kingdom. He is implacably opposed to it. He will always reject everything contaminated with it.

Some people find this difficult to accept. It doesn't seem to square up with their image of a gentle, tolerant God who "is love".

But that is exactly the key to understanding this character of God. He loves us all passionately, more than most people could dream. And he sees sin as the destructive force that destroys life and love. That is *exactly* why he absolutely will not tolerate it – anywhere, anytime, to any degree.

We can easily slip into the way of thinking that God has always seemed obsessed with an arbitrary, clinical code of right and wrong as an end in itself. Not at all! For him, this is all about relationships.

That is why Jesus said that the whole Law – both Godwards and manwards – could be summed up in one thing: **Love**.

God wasn't vexed in the beginning because Adam and Eve had eaten some fruit. The action in itself was not the issue. But he was devastated by their rejection of him as Lord, Creator, the source of all life and blessing. It was a profound breakdown in relationship.

We must always understand Law and obedience in these terms. Even the most seemingly arbitrary ritual laws given to Israel at Sinai had some purpose in terms of relationship: either to help them believe in salvation through one who was to come; or to keep them healthy in a Middle-Eastern climate at a time when people knew very little about germs, diet or medicine.

Because there was so much at stake in those early years after deliverance from Egypt – not only for God's marriage to Israel, but his long-term plans to bring the world into a blessed relationship with him – God would show himself ruthless against all contamination and even the smallest breaches. The issue of obedience was especially critical in those early stages when the nation's new course was being set.[68] God knew, better than anyone, that even small departures could give a foothold to a rebellious spirit that would lead to tremendous suffering for everyone.

---

[68] This is why Ananias and Sapphira were also dealt with so harshly at a similarly critical time in the New Testament church. Cf. Acts 5:1-10.

In the end that's what happened.

To see how God's wrath is inseparable from his passionate love, like two sides of a coin, we need only read the Old Testament prophets, including the twelve so-called minor ones. We hear them crying out with God's voice when things had gone horribly wrong. There he speaks passionately as one whose love has been wilfully slighted, over and over again, in the face of kindness, mercy and blessings. He appeals to the Israelites. He threatens them. He appeals again. He gives them chances time after time. And only when all else fails, heartbroken, does he abandon them to their self-chosen ways.

And even then, not forever....

In the darkest prophetic passages of great sadness and failure, there come bright rays of hope. Because God *will* have them back if they return to him.

That's what repentance is. Turning away from things that displease a loving God. Turning back to a proper relationship with him.

If they do, he will run out to meet them, with tears of joy and wide open arms, like the father in the parable of the prodigal son. He won't hold their sins against them. He will quickly forgive and forget.

Forgiveness and Punishment

God's impassioned message through the Old Testament Prophets clearly shows what forgiveness is:

Not holding our past failures against us.

Instead of exacting vengeance for wronged love, God will have us back into his family, bless us, give us life in place of death. All we need to do is turn around, and turn back.

So why do we insist on the idea that sin has to be punished before it can be forgiven and forgotten? Everything we learn from the Bible about forgiveness speaks of the opposite – of *not* demanding the "pound of flesh"![69]

The idea of necessary punishment in response to law-breaking is one that has crept into our doctrines along with an understanding of *justification* as the settling of a guilty debt through "penal substitution" (i.e. Jesus' death on the Cross).

Anselm, the Archbishop of Canterbury (1093-1109) has a lot to answer for in this respect. He seems to have introduced the highly influential feudal notion of the need to

---

[69] It is true there was a lot of teaching in the Old Testament about blood sacrifices for sin. But with proper New Testament understanding, we can see that this is about cleansing and restoring – not about punishment. That is how the writer of Hebrews teaches it. *Cleansing* and *holiness* are the two major emphases in his analysis of Old Testament rituals and their fulfilment in Christ.

give God "satisfaction" because of wrongs done against him. That was understood to be why Jesus had to be "punished" – to satisfy God's offended honour.[70]

But it's hard to get away from C. S. Lewis' question in "Mere Christianity":

> "If God was prepared to let us off, why on earth did He not do so? And what possible point could there be in punishing an innocent person instead? None at all that I can see, if you are thinking of punishment in the police-court sense."[71]

At this stage, theologians will quote verses which seem to say that God had no choice (because of his justice) but to punish sin, rather than merely forgive it. But of course, if you start off with a theory where *penal substitution = justification = forgiveness of sins*, then you can find verses everywhere which you can read in that light. We will examine some of these below.

But let's reflect for a moment that when God calls us to forgive each other if things go wrong between us, there is no

---

[70] *"Cur Deus homo? There the English saint had proclaimed the picturesque views of Christ defeating the devil and death passé and had invented instead a logical description (highly suggestive of feudal codes of honour) where the Fall, which resulted in robbing God of honor and heaven of the perfect number of beatific inhabitants, necessitated human payment of honor in blood that only God could satisfy."* Wengert, Defending Faith, p 84.

[71] C. S. Lewis (1952) Mere Christianity. Touchstone edition (New York) 1960, p 59.

hint of the need for punishment to settle the score and "satisfy honour". Forgiveness means the opposite: we don't hold things on record against our neighbor or our brother. We don't seek "satisfaction". Instead of exacting vengeance we want to do them good. And we want to enjoy a restored relationship with them.

... *Provided they will let us.*

If they refuse, and want to keep obstacles in the way, that's another story.[72] And this principle shows clearly that forgiveness is not the same as reconciliation.

Having a forgiving heart – holding out the offer of forgiveness – is something we must always do, as God does. But it may not always lead to reconciliation. That is something different. But the ultimate goal of forgiveness is the repair of a relationship.

And that's where the Cross comes in. Our relationship with God needed to be repaired. That is the important thing. The obstacles to our fellowship with him needed to be got out of the way. The Cross is not about settling scores and clearing accounts. It is about reconciliation.

Restoring our fellowship is why Jesus had to die. We couldn't repair things ourselves. We couldn't overcome sin

---

[72] Matthew 18:15-16. Cf. 2 Thess. 3:13-15.

in our lives. And God will not accept us with any taint of sin. His righteous standards are inviolable in that sense.[73]

Only a sinless man could do what needed to be done. In that sense Jesus "died for our sins" – the righteous for the unrighteous. Not because God had to kill someone in order to satisfy his anger – even an innocent person! (No wonder Christian thinkers such as C. S. Lewis and Steve Chalke have had problems with this doctrine, thus understood.)

God shows his forgiving heart for mankind by offering the Cross. The death of Jesus is not the *grounds* for forgiveness in God's heart.[74] But it is what we needed for restoration – our atonement with God. It has put away our sinfulness,[75] which God could not tolerate in a relationship with him.

The Cross, with the resurrection, is God's means of reconciliation. It is the way he provides to bring us back into his family. It is our cleansing, our spiritual adoption, the

---

[73] Cf. *Unless your righteousness exceeds that of the Scribes and Pharisees you will never enter the Kingdom of heaven.* Matthew 5:20.

[74] Because it *shows* his forgiveness, the Cross may be referred to by New Testament writers in ways that can seem to suggest that.

[75] New Testament writers use the words "sins" and "sin" interchangeably to refer to the same thing: our sinfulness i.e. our sinful nature. If we continue to see "sins" as different from "sin" we will gravitate mostly towards a view of the Cross as punishment, a clearing away of guilt rather than of sinfulness itself. Our focus will tend to be on notional records and accounts rather than on real life-change and relationship.

beginning of a new blessed, godly life for us, our redemption from captivity to sin, our deliverance from "him who has the power of death".[76]

In those senses, Jesus "died for our sins". He took on real human nature in a fallen world ("the likeness of sinful flesh", but without sin himself) and engaged in a fight to the death with sin and the devil – the fight which Adam had lost in the beginning.

An analogy might help us understand. By sharing our human nature, Jesus inherited a deadly virus, in common with the rest of mankind (he was made "sin"). But he was also born with the unique immunity which all his life rendered that virus inactive (he had no sin). Because of his divine spirit, he was the only man alive with the antidote to defeat the deadly evil.

Jesus' life was a mission to fight the killer human virus of sin to the bitter end. He was able to overcome sin in our flesh, in human nature, so that he could give us his spirit with its tried and tested cure for the sickness. When we accept it, we receive his new life; and sin receives its death sentence (which is surely what is meant when it says he "condemned sin in the flesh"[77]).

---

[76] Hebrews 2:14.

[77] Romans 8:3.

You have heard it said...

(2) Declarative Righteousness

In this context I need to say a word about what the theologians call "declarative righteousness".

Much has been said and written about the scriptural word translated as "reckoned" e.g. in Abraham's case, "He believed God and God reckoned it to him as righteousness." This is the basis of the so-called forensic view of justification: God *declares* us to be righteous, because of Christ's merits, his work, his righteousness. A righteous status is somehow "imputed" to us. This is salvation based on a system of accounts and credits.

There are several weaknesses in this theory which we will explore in some detail. But first, it is worth noting that this central, Reformed doctrine was born out of great dissatisfaction with Roman Catholic teaching whereby the doctrine of righteousness in actual experience had become abused and distorted. It was presented in such a way as to undermine the paramount notion that salvation is by God's grace alone.

To avoid any confusion about merits, therefore, most

leaders of the Reformation emphasized that righteousness is not something we earn or can possess except by association with Christ.

This is of course a vital, fundamental truth.

But to ensure further that there was no confusion of Christ's righteousness with man's participation, the Reformers placed the entire focus of righteousness external to our experience: in Christ apart from man, in some notional, heavenly courtroom. God's righteous verdict (our being pronounced righteous) had nothing to do (it was said) with actual experience. It was not about our transformation – at least not initially.

This led to the predominant notion still with us today that God only "regards" us as righteous, because of Jesus. You find this cropping up repeatedly in modern songs: "When he looks at me, he sees Jesus" etc. There is a strong implication from the very beginning that our own spiritual transformation is only of secondary importance in the grand scheme of salvation – a nice extra, even an inevitable implication, but not the primary, essential thing.

This, I think, is the real problem with the idea of "justification" that depends on a theory of "penal substitution". It makes God seem more interested

- in accounts, than in people
- in legal status, than in spiritual realities

- in transactions, rather than relationships

Of course the great Reformers were men of the Bible, and you can't read far in the New Testament writings without coming across a huge emphasis on our salvation being worked out in real life (not just written into an account book). This then spawned a vast quantity of Reformed writings about how we acquire the related benefits of salvation in our experience.

To tie the strands together, for example, there has been much teaching about our "union" with Christ, through which we obtain all the blessings that are due to him as a righteous man – first forensically (like a legal verdict) then in varying degrees and at various stages, in our actual possession.

But despite the many theological tomes written about it, it all remains a bit vague and unconvincing. How exactly are we "joined" with him? There can't be any real union except an actual spiritual one. "He that is joined to the Lord is one Spirit with him." All purely *forensic* talk of "reckoning, regarding etc " surely falls down at this point. We are one with him because he is in us and we are in him. He is our life, our righteousness and holiness.

Why was it felt there was a need to distinguish between imputed and imparted[78] righteousness? It was a false

---

[78] Imputed = reckoned to us because of Christ's merits, but only on account, so to

dichotomy which arose out of concern that grace would be undermined (as was happening in the Catholic church) and that people would fail to see that salvation is entirely by faith.

But it needn't be so. God's gift of righteousness *in* me is every bit as undeserved, dependent on faith, and due to grace as the so-called forensic righteousness which is primarily a supposed legal verdict.

And most importantly – from the pastoral point of view – a forensic view of righteousness drives a wedge from the very beginning between the doctrinal basis of our salvation and our experience and expectations in this life. If we are only "regarded" or "reckoned" to be righteous, we are given a weaker footing for our Christian life from the outset. And no matter how much teaching there is about spiritual blessings flowing from that legal position, we are somehow left with the deep, unavoidable feeling that everything else (other than *forensic* righteousness) is ultimately secondary, and less sure.

In the course of the great 16th century dispute with Osiander over the meaning of *justification*, the fight to safeguard "forensic" righteousness seemed to make Luther's followers and Calvinists increasingly extreme in formulating their "*As if…*" theology.

---

speak (a *legal fiction*) ; imparted = made essentially righteous, in experience and reality.

> "Imputation does not mean to be so in truth but to be accepted, held and thus reckoned by God as such, as if it were even as it should be."[79]

And whereas Luther had said, "The entire life that true-believing Christians lead after baptism is nothing more than waiting for the revelation of the blessedness that they already possess. They certainly have it completely..." (cited in Wengert, ibid p 286), Pollicarius, in opposing Osiander, said "that the divine righteousness in us was only imputed and that we were awaiting the coming of the essential righteousness" in the next life.[80] So, effectively, all we can hope to be in this life is forgiven.

This view of life has traditionally been backed up by a misreading of the struggling believer in Romans 7 and lurks today at the back of many Christians' minds.[81] I am not arguing that we can be perfect before the resurrection. But a proper reading of Paul's letter to the Romans surely gives us a very positive picture of the normal Christian life as one of power and victorious freedom.

What then of all the texts which seem to speak of righteousness in purely forensic terms (pronounced,

---

[79] Mörlin in his "Bericht", quoted in Wengert, Defending Faith, p 109. Similarly Flacius interpreted 2 Peter 1:4 to refer only to our transformation in the coming age (Wengert ibid, p 140) - as did Calvin (cf. Institutes, Vol 2, p 46).

[80] Wengert ibid, p 287.

[81] Cf. Calvin, Institutes Vol 2, p 48.

reckoned, declared, regarded)? Is that really something distinct from our spiritual transformation in reality?

An analogy might help us here. At an awards ceremony, say at a teacher training college, the roll call of honours will be read, and the happy students will be awarded their diplomas. They are then qualified teachers. But in this ceremony they are declared to be teachers because they have done the training. The certificate only testifies to the skills and competences that they now have. Of course they are not perfect and they will have much to learn. But they are qualified as teachers because that is what they are.

None of us would want our children to be taught by teachers who were merely "reckoned" to be teachers – perhaps because of a nepotistic parent who happened to be the college president! In the same way, God does not want his heaven to be peopled with citizens whom he can only "regard" as righteous.

No analogy is perfect. What is true in our example in the natural world gives way to something more startling in the supernatural realm. We get our "certificate of righteousness" because Jesus Christ has done the necessary training for us – and he transfuses the benefits of his life's experiences, complete, mature and perfect, into our hearts and minds.

"He learned obedience through the things he suffered. And being made perfect he became the source of

eternal salvation for all those who obey him."[82]

He gives us his perfection.[83]

So when God declares us to be righteous, that is in fact what he makes us.

- When God says "Let there be light", there is light.
- When God says "Get up and walk", a man gets up and walks.
- When God says, "Be righteous", he gives us his Spirit.

Jesus said, "The words that I speak to you are spirit and life." The power is in the words. They bring about the spiritual change that they speak of in their message – provided they meet with faith. The gospel, says Paul, is the "*power* of God unto salvation".

> **"So shall my word be that goes out from my mouth; it shall not return to me empty, but it shall accomplish that which I purpose, and shall succeed in the thing for which I sent it."**[84]

---

[82] Hebrews 5:9.

[83] *Perfection* is a major leitmotif in the book of Hebrews. Our attaining this through Jesus' perfect life is something about which the writer says he has much to explain (5:11) which would be hard for his hearers. It is not the role of Melchizedek which he says he has difficult things to say about. The text might lead you to read it like that.

[84] Isaiah 55:11.

Everything past, present and future comes
- from the Father
- through the Word, his Son
- by the Spirit.

The Spirit of God's power is in the Word and brings us the grace contained in the message.

This is why when we pray or sing, we offer thanks
- to the Father
- through Jesus Christ ("in his name")
- because of what the Spirit has done.

In the end, all the glory goes back to God for his mercies.

So if we emphasize an *imparted* righteousness rather than a *forensic* one, let us be clear that

- It is no less an *entirely* free gift of God.

- It is no less *perfect* if we sometimes fail to live it out perfectly.

- It is no less an *eternal guarantee* of blessing because it is placed within us.

There is no need, pastorally or theologically, to see our righteousness as a two-part process – first legal, then experienced. God has spoken. He has declared us to be righteous – and that is what he makes us, by the Spirit, through Christ.

You have heard it said...

(3) Proof-Texts and Fantasies

Meanwhile the idea of "penal substitution" has spawned a whole gamut of misunderstandings, bad Scripture translations, and fantastic notions which people may readily tend to accept as "gospel".

Proof-Texts

(i) 1 Peter 2:14
Firstly, let's be clear and honest that one of the main "proof-texts" used to show Jesus' death as punishment for sins, is based on a serious mistranslation. Yet it is a text held to be so central to Reformed ideas of "penal substitution" and "justification" that modern translators seem afraid to render it any differently.

Here is how it should read:

> *He himself carried our sins in his body <u>up</u> <u>onto</u> the wood (i.e. cross).*

Not –

> *He himself bore our sins in his body on the wood (cross).*

The Greek is absolutely plain. It is not that somehow God the Father, there and then, dumped all the world's sins onto Jesus when he was hanging on that Roman cross. His whole life long Jesus had been carrying our "sins", in his assumed "likeness of sinful flesh" – and now he was approaching the last stage, the climactic, harrowing setting for the ultimate victory. He was carrying human nature up towards its final crucifixion. *Up onto the cross...* The solution had to be radical. And in the end, nothing could have been more extreme.

* * * * * * * * * * * *

(ii) Then there is this verse:

> ***Christ redeemed us from the curse of the Law by becoming a curse for us. For it is written, Cursed is everyone who hangs on a tree.* Galatians 3:13**

It will help us understand this truth accurately if we ask ourselves, "When did this happen? When did Jesus bear our human curse?" And the startling answer is: All his life, from the very beginning to the Cross.

Paul points to the crucifixion as the most extreme evidence of this truth: "cursed is everyone who hangs on a tree". But the Cross was only the final, appalling chapter in a whole life in which Jesus bore Adam's curse in his human body.

It can still shock us to think like this, but Jesus was part of our fallen humanity. He was one of us. This is the very foundation of our salvation.[85]

Through Mary, Jesus inherited Adam's fallen humanity – yet was immune to it – so that as our liberator he could bring us out of our fallen (cursed) state and into glorious resurrection life. His body was mortal because of Adam, and because of Mary, but his spirit was righteous and alive. Paul says that with Jesus' spirit in us, we live with the same duality:

> **"On the one hand the body is dead because of sin, on the other hand the Spirit is life because of righteousness."**[86]

Jesus was therefore the representative of the Old Adam and of the New Adam at the same time. He was human and divine. He was in sinful flesh but without sin. He was born under the curse, yet the curse could not hold him. He could have walked away from it at any time. "A curse that is causeless does not alight."[87]

---

[85] Roman Catholicism can tend to erode this foundational truth by insisting on special purifying grace for Mary, and even Mary's mother (!) to prepare for Jesus' sinlessness.

[86] Romans 8:10.

[87] Proverbs 26:2.

Instead he chose to live our shared human lot to its very end, suffering the worst of deaths on a cross. Voluntarily. Not as punishment – but to wrench final victory from sin and free mankind from mortality.

To understand these mysteries properly, we need to read Galatians 3:13 in the light of other passages that talk of Jesus' mission in similar terms.

- God sending his own son *in the likeness of sinful flesh* and for sin,[88] condemned sin the flesh.

- God sent forth his son, born of a woman, *born under the Law*, to redeem those under the Law (Galatians 4:4).

- Since therefore the children share in flesh and blood, he himself likewise *partook of the same nature,* that through death he might destroy him who has the power of death, that is, the devil (Hebrews 2:14).

- Therefore *he had to be made like his brethren in every respect,* so that he might become a merciful and faithful high priest in the service of God to make expiation for the sins of the people (Hebrews 2:17-18).

An analogy might help us understand this.

---

[88] "To be a sin offering" (NIV) is *not* a translation, merely a translator's unwarranted interpretation.

As the *Son of Man*, Jesus was born with our human virus in his flesh. He inherited it. We can call the virus A.D.A.M.(1) – Anti-Divine Acquired Mortality. But Jesus was also a new sort of Adam, the prototype of a different humanity. In his new nature (one nature, not two) he had the only anti-virus which could save us from sin and death's curse: A.D.A.M.(2) – Active Divinity Against Mortality. (I must ask the reader to bear with me for I am trying to explain the almost inexplicable!) He had these both at the same time. Mortality and immortality – the blessing of life and the curse of death.

In the beginning, God had proclaimed that sin, the breakdown in relationship with him, would lead to death. Suffering and death was its curse, and life is God's blessing. This Ancient Covenant is re-stated by Paul when he summarizes the code of Law Israel later received at Sinai (Galatians 3:10): ***Keep it and you will live. Break it and you will die.***

Jesus, as the new man, had to undo Adam's wrongdoing to restore a proper relationship. He could only achieve this by doing what was absolutely right before God.

- **Where Adam wanted to place himself at the centre, Jesus gave up everything in love.**[89]

---

[89] Philippians 2:6-8.

- **Where Adam abandoned faith in God, Jesus held unto to it under the most extreme testing circumstances.**[90]

- **Where the devil beguiled Adam with false promises, Jesus would not give in, even when Satan's agents tortured him.**[91]

Jesus resisted the global pandemic virus of sin to the bitter end. He could have walked away from it, unscathed, back into heaven. Instead he embraced his lot as a man in an evil world, to overcome, rise out of it, and free us from it. His death therefore was
- the killing of sin
- the annulling of the curse
- the death of death
- the end of the rule of the prince of darkness.

The Cross was the end-game. Throughout his whole life Jesus had been engaged in this battle with sin and its curse. The virus and the anti-virus had been in Jesus' nature since he was an embryo in Mary's womb. On the Cross, the victory was final.

When we read passages in Hebrews about Jesus being tempted "in every respect the way we are", we have come to

---

[90] Hebrews 5:7-8 and 12:2.

[91] 1 Peter 2:21-23 and 4:1-2.

regard this as a sort of *extra* in our salvation story. We find it comforting that he knows what we are going through etc.

But the truth of Jesus' perfect struggle against sin is not a nice extra. It *is* our salvation. It constitutes the essence of human redemption.

That is what the writer of Hebrews tried to show using the metaphor of High Priesthood (Jesus "interceding" for us *etc*). In today's parlance for a modern audience, we might talk in the language of prototypes. The Hebrews writer himself switches from liturgical imagery to describing Jesus as the *author*, or *founder* and *perfecter* of our faith. But he is saying the same thing. Jesus' life representing all mankind was both the end of the old humanity and the beginning of a new redeemed race.

Jesus' extreme obedience settled the whole issue of the Law and its demands. Perfect love, under the greatest duress, had been honoured by the new man. As the writer of Hebrews puts it, Jesus was "made perfect" as a man.

The Law, representing man's relationship to God, could not be more perfectly upheld. For that reason it says that Christ is the end of the Law – the fulfilment of it; the last word on it.

So when we take Jesus' death into our lives, the Law's requirements are perfectly accomplished in us, through his Spirit.

In all those senses, Jesus saved man from the broken Law and took away its curse from us by his suffering. Sin was always going to mean suffering and death. But either it would kill man, or one day a man would condemn and kill it… by dying.

Jesus was not bound by the curse of suffering and death resting on humanity, so he was able to voluntarily take it, flip it over and turn it into a different sort of suffering: the curse's undoing, and the death of death.

Athanasius sums it up like this:

> "Thus, taking a body like our own, because all our bodies were liable to the corruption of death, he surrendered his body to death instead of all, and offered it to the Father. This he did out of sheer love for us, so that in his death all might die, and the law of death thereby be abolished."[92]

This was what C. S. Lewis's Aslan described as *the deeper magic*.[93]

* * * * * * * * * * * *

---

[92] The Incarnation of the Word of God, trans. A Religious of C. S. M. V. (London: Geoffrey Bles, 1944) p 35. Cited in "Christ Crucified", Donald Macleod (2014).

[93] C. S. Lewis (1950). The Lion, the Witch and the Wardrobe.

(iii) *Without the shedding of blood there is no remission.* Hebrews 9:22

The writer of Hebrews gives us the best commentary on the Old Testament emphasis on liturgy, holiness and the role of blood in cleansing us. But when we read verses like 9:22, we are conditioned to think of punishment. The writer instead continually emphasizes that blood cleanses us: makes us holy. The sacrifice removes sin from *us* – not from an account. When we are purified, then we can enter God's presence. God wants fellowship with clean people, not with clean sheets!

The Law was our teacher, says Paul, pointing us to Christ. This verse is often used negatively (especially by Lutherans) to mean that the Law showed us how badly we fall short of God's glorious standards.

That is only part of it. "The Law was added because of transgressions", means that it taught men and women about God's righteous standards and, necessarily, the opposite – but also therefore the need for, and the offer of cleansing. Hence the continual emphasis on blood.

In these ways the Law highlighted righteousness, sin, and forgiveness, and pointed Old Testament believers to Christ – in a positive way. As the Hebrews writer eloquently points out, the Law was never meant to be an alternative to salvation through Christ. Quite the opposite: it was meant to support believers' faith in God's grace.

When Christians sing or talk about *blood*, I sometimes wonder if they forget that blood is synecdochical for death (it stands for it) – it is what is called a linguistic *trope*. There is no magical power in blood itself. It is only powerful in so far as it represents a life poured out.

Blood in that sense was always going to be necessary for putting away sin. There was only one basis for mankind's salvation. It was going to be through a death. But not a death as a punishment – rather, a death to free us from sin and make us God's children.

- Jesus sacrifice was a death not to cleanse accounts, but to cleanse people.

- Jesus died to make us holy, so that we could have fellowship with God.[94]

God doesn't want sinless records: he wants sinless people. We could never make ourselves holy enough for fellowship with God. God had to do it for us through Jesus' death.

---

[94] Hebrews 12:14: *Strive for the holiness without which no one will see God.*

The ceremonial rituals under the Old Covenant pointed forward to that great work and focused minds on the fact that a blood sacrifice was necessary to bring and to keep God's people under his blessing.

* * * * * * * * * * * *

(iv) Lastly let us look at another key text that is often quoted to underline the need for penal substitution, as traditionally understood:

> *He did this to show his righteousness, because in his divine forbearance he had passed over the sins previously committed.* **Romans 3:25**

This is taken to mean that God had no choice but to punish someone for sin. He couldn't just forgive. He couldn't act against his justice (we are told).

Therefore in this passage, Paul's cascading, unpunctuated clauses are re-arranged in sentences in such a way as to highlight this point.[95] Translated words are lined up to support traditional doctrine. "Righteousness" as a gracious means of salvation in verse 22 suddenly becomes "justice" in verse 26 (NIV version), even though it is the same Greek word in both places. And predictably, "justified" with its

---

[95] This is another classic case where words like "just/justice/justification" are deliberately alternated with concepts of "righteousness/right/made righteous" (though all from the same root word) and we lose the proper flow in Paul's argument.

inherited legal overtones is offered instead of "made righteous".

But if we read the passage as a unified whole, from verses 21 to 25, we see that in mentioning God's forbearance of "former sins" in the context of salvation, Paul is simply emphasizing that God doesn't let sins stand in the way of saving us: he doesn't hold them against us. He is not arguing that God had to punish Jesus because he had passed over former sins and therefore had to honour his justice by doling out a sentence. He doesn't say that.

We find the same when Paul quotes from David (Romans 4:6-9): "Blessed is the man whose sins are forgiven". He is just emphasizing that blessing is not achieved by observance of the Law. On the contrary, it is obvious that we need forgiveness before we can access blessing. Salvation comes as a free offer of righteousness. We can't earn it by works. David knew that. Paul proclaims it.

That is what the Apostle is saying in both passages in Romans. It is not that God was bound to punish someone with death because he had forgiven sins: simply rather that he forgives and he saves.

You find this same link of free grace and salvation in Paul's words to Titus:

"He saved us not because of deeds done by us in righteousness, but according to his great mercy,

through the washing of rebirth and renewal in the Holy Spirit which he richly poured out on us through Jesus Christ our saviour, so that being made righteous by his grace, we might become heirs according to the hope of eternal life."[96]

... And Fantasies

Meanwhile the notion of all the world's sins suddenly being dumped upon Jesus on the Cross for punishment continues to develop a life of its own, giving rise to all sorts of fanciful (though well-meant) myths.

Here are a few common ones.

The Father turned his face away...

No he didn't!

When Jesus quoted Psalm 22 in his distress,[97] it was a cry of faith and a prayer for deliverance. He was signaling that his was the suffering David had prophesied in that Psalm.

The writer of Hebrews gives us the best commentary

---

[96] Titus 3:5-7

[97] *My God, my God why hast thou forsaken me?*

on it:

> **"In the days of his flesh, he offered up prayers and supplications with loud crying and tears to the one able to save him from death."**[98]

There was never any separation between Jesus and his Father because of sin – any more than David had been separated from God when he wrote those words. We have to remember that the Psalms are emotive, prophetic poetry, not systematic theology.

In quoting the first words, Jesus was invoking the whole Psalm, including its hope:

> "For he has not despised or abhorred the affliction of the afflicted; and he has not hid his face from him, but has heard when he cried to him." [99]

Note: *"He has not hid his face from him..."*

If I could say something foolish, under pressure to reinforce a point (following Paul's example[100]) I would be tempted to say that Jesus and his Father were surely never closer than at that time when he was sacrificing himself in love for a lost mankind.

---

[98] Hebrews 5:7.

[99] Psalm 22:24.

[100] 2 Cor. 11:17.

- **He descended unto hell**

    You cannot build a bizarre doctrine like this out of one verse in a difficult, obscure passage.[101]

    The so-called "Apostles' Creed" was almost certainly not written by any Apostles, and the first mention we have of it is in a letter dated 390 AD.

    This is an old doctrine which I mention here only because I recently heard it used in connection with "penal substitution".

- **The Father poured out his wrath on Jesus for our sins.**

    This is a morbid notion that has crept into popular preaching and many new songs used in churches. But even among conservative evangelicals who uphold some moderate idea of "penal substitution" there is generally no belief that God the Father vented his anger on Jesus. Here is what Howard Marshall says:

---

[101] 1 Peter 3:19. See John Piper's helpful blog at http://www.desiringgod.org/blog/posts/did-jesus-spend-saturday-in-hell--2

> "Where are these evangelicals who say that God punished Christ? Name them! Where are the evangelicals who will repudiate this statement, written by John Calvin: "We do not, however, insinuate that God was ever hostile to him or angry with him." You will not find them among serious theologians, although I recognise that popular preachers may err in this respect..."[102]

When we read prophetic passages such as Isaiah 53, about the Suffering Servant, we have to remember that Jesus and the Father were agreed on this drastic course of action. There was no other way to rescue mankind. In that sense – and only in that sense – did the Father want his Son to be *bruised for our transgressions*: "It was the will of the Lord to bruise him"; not because he felt bound to punish someone in his anger.

There was no way to redeem man other than suffering. This cost had been predicted as early as the Garden of Eden.[103] The "chastisement of our peace was upon him", because death to sin was what it would take to undo the deep damage. The Cross was not about settling God's accounts. It was his way of cleansing us – in our substance, not in a ledger – so that we could enjoy fellowship with him and his blessings.

---

[102] Marshall, H (2008) in Tidball, D., Hilborn, D., and Thacker, J. (eds). The Atonement Debate. Papers from the London Symposium on the Theology of Atonement. Grand Rapids (Mi): Zondervan. P 63.

[103] Genesis 3:15.

Of course, if men and women continue in their sins, disregarding the one who made and loves them, choosing a life on the Enemy's side instead, then God's angry punishment will come upon them, not because he doesn't love them; but because of the deadly evil of sin. You can say that he keeps account in that way. There is a "book of life".

God has inviolable standards of holiness. His "justice" in that sense is non-negotiable. But Jesus didn't die as a punishment for our breaking his Law. He died to ensure that we would become the sort of heavenly citizens who would keep the Law – in his righteousness.

That is what it means to "walk in the Spirit".[104] It is life in the glorious Spirit of Jesus, the second Adam, the perfect Man, who was also divine.

"By loyalty and faithfulness, iniquity is atoned for."[105]

This is our Atonement:

his perfection

...in us.

---

[104] Translators lose the power of this glorious phrase when they translate it as "keep in step with the Spirit"(NIV). It is much more profoundly mystical and existential than that. I dearly wish that translators would stop imposing their paraphrases where there is no need for them!

[105] Proverbs 16:6.

You have heard it said…

(4). "New" Perspectives on Paul

I must say a few words about the so-called "new" Pauline theology which has been attracting attention in theological circles in recent years. This is a technically difficult area and should only be of interest to those who have been exposed to this sort of thinking through N. T. Wright or others. (Otherwise you might like to skip this section.)

I think that a major problem with the *New Perspectives on Paul* (NPP) school of thought is precisely its tendency to lose perspective.

Typically, NPP teachers will look at a passage which people turn to for truth about grace and personal salvation, and they will say, "No, it's not about grace or personal salvation. It's about God's covenantal promises." They move the focus from the picture to its frame. They shift our attention from the end goal of salvation to ecclesiological strategies. They criticize the Reformers for what they consider to be an unbalanced reading of Paul's letters.

But in so far as Reformed theologians have kept the central emphasis on core realities, they must surely have been right. In so far as NPP exponents have placed the main emphasis on covenantal frameworks, they miss the point. If we are going to err in any direction, surely it is better to focus on the wonderful results of salvation rather than dispensational parameters. I have heard one NPP exponent deliver three seminars on Romans without once mentioning the Holy Spirit. There is surely something amiss with such an approach.

Having hit on some interesting views of scriptural passages by looking through a particular scholarship prism, NPP proponents will typically want to see everything else through that one prism. The result is a strangely distorted view of the big picture.

A doctrinaire approach develops. NPP proponents will sometimes go to extraordinary lengths to explain away the obvious meaning of texts to try to fit everything into their schemata.[106] You are often left with something that doesn't feel intuitively right. It lacks the straightforwardness – as well as the man-centredness – of the many texts which speak of Christ's coming

> "to save the people from their sins"
> "to destroy the works of the devil"
> "to bring many sons to glory"
>   etc.

---

[106] Cf. The example of J. Dunn trying to avoid the clear, universal meaning of the "curse" in Galatians 3:10-14, referenced in O'Kelley (2014), Did the Reformers Misread Paul? p 123 ff.

Sometimes with NPP you could almost take away the impression that Jesus' mission was about God justifying himself, rather than saving mankind!

The safest way of maintaining Biblical perspective, in my understanding, is to see "covenant" as meaning relationship. The end of all God's workings with mankind is a real, personal, spiritual relationship with God as our Father.

Therefore there has only really ever been one "covenant" between God and man. It is the ancient one that has been from the beginning: "Desire God's love, and you will live. Reject him and you will die." All subsequent formulations of this Ancient Covenant (Abraham, Sinai, New Testament) must be seen in that context. This will help keep our focus on the important things.

Life is all about relationship within God's family. God's unchanging purpose is to share his eternal glory by extending his heavenly family. After Eden, he has also had to deal in various ways with grave new problems (sin, Satan's control, death) – but the ultimate goal has never changed. Fellowship between God and man is forever the most important focus.

NPP's attempts to re-focus on the covenantal aspects of Paul's writings can leave you with the impression that understanding covenantal nuances is more important than the redemptive results of God's salvation plan. Of course there shouldn't be any dichotomy. But there is a big question of balance and emphasis.

God's successive, changing dispensations are all designed to save many individuals and form them into one holy nation, God's family. And this can only happen individually. NPP tends to over-emphasize God's global purposes, in reaction to traditional Catholic and Protestant tendencies to read about individual salvation. But God's strategy is "to bring many sons to glory". That can only happen one by one.

There is also much talk in NPP of "status" and "standing", and not enough emphasis, in my view, on real individual spiritual transformation which is at the heart of it all.

For example, although according to NPP the word "righteousness" may have been used to describe God's actions within the context of previous covenants, it is surely more primal and existential than that. God's righteousness is his eternal character. The obvious corollary of his being righteous is the need for each individual to acquire that same spirit of righteousness as the basis for fellowship with him. As a father, I am not interested in my children's *status* or *standing* within our family: I am interested in a loving relationship with them. Relationship is communion. That is what God wants.

NPP may have some interesting things to say about first-century understanding of covenantal frameworks. But they can deflect our focus away from our personal relationship with God, based on individual righteousness and holiness through his Holy Spirit. There is a great risk that through this they will leave believers spiritually confused and undernourished.

That, I think, is the real danger of NPP.

Did the Reformers Misread Paul?

If you want to go more deeply into the New Perspective debate, read Aaron O'Kelley's fairly balanced study "Did the Reformers Misread Paul?"[107]

First-century Judaism may have been (technically) a religion of grace, as E.P. Sanders[108] influentially argued – but then so was late Medieval Catholicism, says O'Kelley. The distortion of doctrines of grace by the Catholic Church led Luther to cry out for a sanitized "gospel", one where "works" had no part to play in securing salvation. Could this not have been the same for Paul, when faced with a "covenantal nomism"[109] gone badly wrong?

Doctrinally, and in practice, an attempted fusion of works, merits and grace is very difficult to get right. Agreed, therefore, there may theoretically have been *grace* in first century Jewish religion; but in practice, the Sinaitic covenant had become a barrier for many to true relationship with God in faith and love.

---

[107] Did the Reformers Misread Paul? (2014).

[108] Paul and Palestinian Judaism. E. P. Sanders (1977).

[109] This is Sanders' phrase, signifying a positive place for law-keeping within the framework of a covenant of grace.

That is why Paul had to speak out against its abuse – as Luther had done in the Catholic church context.

God has always wanted a loving relationship with men and women as his children. And that is precisely where it can go wrong: when men start substituting doctrines, spiritless law-observation, covenantal "standing" and frameworks in place of a trusting, loving, personalized relationship with the living God.

It is spiritual reality that God wants. Faced with a badly skewed "covenantal nomism" of the first century, Paul can only have been writing so urgently about "anthropological and soteriological reality"[110] rather than primarily about "sociological and ecclesiological" contexts, as supposed by new perspective exponents, says O'Kelley.

---

[110] Did the Reformers Misread Paul? O'Kelley, p 117.

You have heard it said...

(5). "Justification" and "Sanctification"

Over the years, much has been said and written in Protestant theology about these two words. "Justification" as a single, external, forensic transaction has been contrasted with "sanctification" as something worked out in actual experience and over time.

These distinctions I find to be unnecessary and unhelpful, though I admit I myself believed them for many years. They support a view whereby the act of "justification" emphasized by Paul in Romans 3-5 is seen as categorically different from the outworked results of it in chapters 6-8.

Having created this artificial split, theologians are then at great pains to show how these things hang together. But the cracks show. The explanations are never very convincing.

To be "justified" simply means to be "made righteous". I believe this means being transformed: made righteous by renewal in our essential nature. Paul uses this terminology a lot.

To be "sanctified" through Jesus' blood simply means to be "made holy". The writer of Hebrews more often speaks with this language of cleansing and purification. This is because his particular aim was to wean Jewish believers off dependence on the ceremonial laws of the Old Covenant. Paul's emphasis was more on universal, moral standards of righteous life according to the Law.

In both cases the writers teach that the transformation is instantaneous, unrepeatable, and irrevocable. In both cases righteousness/holiness is the free blessing which is ours through Jesus' death.

The writer of Hebrews repeatedly links this transformation of the believer with being "made perfect". The perfection he says Jesus won for us through obedient endurance as a man is given to us by his Spirit. The writer talks therefore about "the spirits of righteous men *made perfect*". He says that "by a single offering he has *perfected* for all time those being sanctified".[111]

In parallel, in Romans, Paul explains how Jesus' lifelong obedience, culminating in the ultimate sacrifice, undid Adam's sinful legacy in man.[112] Jesus, as a perfect man, can therefore make us perfect with his righteousness.

We have the holy, perfect, righteous life of Jesus in us. When we receive the Spirit of Jesus, we receive the Spirit of

---

[111] Hebrews 10:14. And see the link in Hebrews 10:1-2 between being made perfect and being cleansed from sin.

[112] Romans 5:18-19.

his death and his resurrection. That is our purification, the end of our old unrighteousness, and the beginning of our new life. We are then *in* the second Adam, and he is in us.

Righteousness and holiness become ours in an instant through spiritual rebirth. You find both concepts (being purified and being made right) shown to be the results of spiritual rebirth in these words from Paul to Titus:

> **"He saved us by the *washing* of regeneration and renewal in the Holy Spirit, so that being made *righteous*… we would become heirs in hope of eternal life."**[113]

Having been transformed, of course we should expect to live out the rest of our lives as changed people. This is then the ongoing dimension that shapes our daily living. On the basis of our new identity Paul calls us to "put to death the deeds of the old nature" by the Spirit. For

> **"How can we who died to sin still live in it?"**[114]

We won't always do it perfectly. Paul knew that; that's why he said he himself wasn't yet perfect.[115] But we have the perfect life of Jesus within us.

---

[113] Titus 3:5.

[114] Romans 6:2.

[115] Philippians 3:12.

Being made righteous ("justified") and being made holy ("sanctified") are two sides of a penny. They are different ways of describing the new godly nature we have when we receive Jesus' perfect Spirit.

Renewal is a free gift of God. It is instantaneous *and* it has an ongoing dimension. Once we have this blessing of godly life, we naturally find ourselves living it out, as taught in Romans 6 and 8 by Paul, and urged repeatedly by the writer of the book of Hebrews (3:12; 4:11). It is inaccurate to say that "justification" is a one-off transaction whereas "sanctification" is a lifelong process.

* * * * * * * * * * * * * *

Our old nature is past history. We have become a new creation.

But we still exist in this world. We find ourselves living with dualism this side of the resurrection, and we may therefore get into difficulties as we seek to live out this new heavenly life.

Romans 7 shows how and why things go wrong. We can learn some salutary lessons from the struggles depicted in that famous seventh chapter. We will look at these in the following section.

You have heard it said...

(6). Romans 7 – The Controversial "Man"

The glorious Spirit-filled life of freedom depicted in Romans 6 and 8[116] seems to stand in stark contrast to the struggles of the "man" in Romans 7 who tries in vain to live a godly life (7:14-24). Here we meet someone who is trying to reform himself focused on the written code of the Law, whereas what is needed is spiritual power.

But who exactly is this struggling person who wants to be good but can't? Is it Paul writing autobiographically?

Martin Lloyd-Jones says that Romans Chapter 7 has proved to be one of the most controversial passages in the whole Bible. Certainly over the years, the greatest Christian thinkers have racked their brains trying to understand what Paul is saying there.

The central question is whether the struggles of the "man" should be read as the normal Christian life (as exemplified in Paul´s own experience) – or is it a case of something having gone badly wrong.

---

[116] *Sin will have no dominion over you, since you are not under law but under grace* (6:14)... *in order that the just requirements of the law might be met in us who walk not according to the flesh but according to the Spirit* (8:4).

Lloyd-Jones, in his landmark exposition of Romans, proves quite convincingly, in my view, that the struggles depicted in Chapter 7 *cannot* be read as the normal Christian life.[117] If Romans 7:14-24 is a picture of how things actually are in our lives, then something has gone wrong.

He offers an alternative interpretation. This is a person, he suggests, who is still unredeemed and unspiritual (cf. 7:14 "I am carnal; sold under sin") but one on whom the Spirit has started to work with conviction of sin, so that the person can at least say, "I delight in the Law of God in my inmost self."

One problem with this interpretation is that it seems to go against what Lloyd-Jones himself emphasizes elsewhere in his exposition of Romans chapters 5-8. He states categorically that there are only two types of people in the world: those who have no interest in pleasing God, and those who are alive to God and want to; those who are spiritually righteous, and those who are "carnal". It is either-or. There is no half-way house.

Is this then after all a *third* sort of person described by Lloyd-Jones – someone who is, as it were, half converted?[118]

---

[117] M. Lloyd-Jones (1973). Romans. Exposition of Chapters 7:1 - 8:4. Cf. pp 192 - 195; and 239-243

[118] Compare his statement on p 256 (ibid): *"But for a time they are in this position, as it were, of being neither the one nor the other, neither unregenerate nor regenerate"* – with these words on p 84: *"we are reminded of the completeness of the change. You are either a Christian or not a Christian; you cannot be partly*

But could such a person really say (without being regenerated) "It is no longer I who sin but sin that dwells within me"? I don't think so.

I think the clear key to understanding the struggles described in Romans 7 is given in verses 5-6. Here we find a summary of two different lifestyles, one under Law, and the other in the Spirit:

> " While we *were* living in the flesh (*in the past, not now*) our sinful passions aroused by the Law, were at work in our members to bear fruit for death. (*This is the syndrome he describes in detail in 7:14-24*).
> **But now** (*signals a change*) we are discharged... so that we serve not under the old written code but in the new life of the spirit (*so the previous helpless scenario need no longer apply to us*).[119]

The sad struggles and failures described in verses 7:14-24, summarized again in 7:25 b (which is not a conclusion) therefore cannot be viewed as the normal Christian experience.

Instead, the message here, and throughout these chapters in Romans, is clear and consistent. Men and women on their own cannot make themselves essentially better, even when

---

Christian. You are either "dead" or "alive"; you are either "born" or "not born". Becoming a Christian is not a gradual process..."

[119] Romans 7: 5-6.

they know God's requirements. When they try, they can end up worse than before.[120] *But* the radical alternative we now enjoy is spiritual transformation: new life. Walk in the Spirit: that is the powerful solution which leads to life and peace.

It seems however that it is possible even for converted Christians to fall back into a carnal way of life through a faulty relationship to the Law. We find this in one of Paul's other letters, when the Galatians were thinking of reverting to Mosaic rituals.

> **"Are you so foolish? Having begun with the Spirit, are you now ending with the flesh?"**[121]

Similarly, after believers in Corinth had begun their spiritual life, Paul felt he still had to call some of them "carnal" because of their behaviour:

> **"And I brothers was not able to speak to you as to spiritual men, but as to carnal, infants in Christ... you are still carnal."**[122]

In view of these texts, it could be argued that the struggling person in Romans 7, whom Paul describes as "carnal", captive to sin, was someone who had once had a

---

[120] Luke 11:43-45.

[121] Galatians 3:3.

[122] 1 Corinthians 3:1-3.

genuine Christian experience (*I once lived without the Law*, 7:9), but then became de-railed through the re-imposition of spiritless Law as the misguided driving force in his/her life.[123]

I was very heartened to read that this was also the conclusion Derek Prince had come to after many years of grappling with the meaning of this enigmatic seventh chapter of Romans.[124]

Derek also says that in his view, falling back into legalism (Law without Spirit) is *the* greatest danger facing believers – at least as regards daily living, if not as a determinant of their ultimate destiny.[125]

The lesson for us all is clear: power to change comes only from the Spirit within us. That is the basis of our mystical daily relationship with God, which is the source of our joy, peace, motivation and strength. We must never lose sight of that. We must cultivate it and feed on it every day.

If sincere believers find their Christian walk to be a constant struggle and they seem to be losing the battle

---

[123] Another possibility, though unlikely, is that Paul is talking allegorically on behalf of Israel. Certainly, legalism had become an endemic problem in Israel in the latter years leading up to Christ's coming. It hadn´t always been like that.

[124] By Grace Alone, published by Derek Prince Ministries, 2013, p 60.

[125] Ibid p 60.

against sin, there is only one possible reason, according to Paul in Romans. Without realizing it, they have slipped back under Law. Something has blocked the enjoyable, liberating flow of the Spirit in their lives and the wonderful sense of closeness to God in fellowship which that brings. Law's demands and religious forms have begun to replace an intimate relationship with God.

Then sin starts getting something of its old power back.

Law, guilt, weakness – a downward spiral

The problems start with a blurred focus.

When we concentrate doctrinally almost exclusively on issues of guilt and forgiveness, we can end up surprisingly weak. We lose sight of the radical change that has taken place in us by his spiritual power. The very "gospel" that seems to celebrate "grace" so resoundingly can start to lead us subtly away from grace, back under the letter of the Law and into a vicious circle of weakness and guilt, (Romans 7: 14-24).

The result can be a long-term sense of failure and worthlessness – sure signs of an unhealthy relationship to the Law. This spiritual depression can lead to reactions in two very different directions:

(i) There can be a sudden reversion to bad old habits. As

people seek to compensate for the lack of fulfilment they feel in their lives, they may start turning back to the sort of reckless behaviour they thought they had left behind.

- *By contrast, when we enjoy daily spiritual fellowship with God, we automatically show fruits of the Spirit like goodness, gentleness, self-control.*

(ii) More subtly, an inner barrenness caused by focusing on the letter of the Law may be concealed for a long time. Some people maintain a religious veneer. The danger then is that this unhealthy relationship to the Law leads to censorious and hypocritical formalism.

- *By contrast, what God wants for us is a life of joy, peace, and love as we "walk in the Spirit".*

To understand why there are these two opposite reactions to Law without Spirit, we simply have to see that some people are genetically more self-disciplined than others. Or they may come from more stable home environments. When the letter of the Law starts to replace spiritual life in their case, instead of resorting to wild self-gratification, a cold, spiritless legalism can develop. Meanwhile the problem of sin is merely internalized.

That is not the answer, though it may look better on the outside. Perhaps this is why Paul chose to focus in Romans 7 on a commandment about wrong desires, rather than outward behaviour, when he was depicting the struggles of someone living under the Law.[126]

Why does the letter of the Law have such dire effects on us?

Why is it that Law without Spirit seems to make sin more virulent in our lives, even after we have become believers?

Of course there is an obvious reason: the spirit of sin in our old nature wants to preserve its last days. It will fight back for its (residual) existence, unless it is replaced with something more positive – the life of the Spirit. That is Paul's solution to the "works of the flesh" in Galatians 5. Replace the old nature with heavenly life and love. Concentrate on enjoying the positive life.

There are other subtle factors that make sin a potent force if we fixate on the letter of the Law without the Spirit. It is helpful to be aware of them. Forewarned is forearmed. I will try to unpick some of these.

(i) We lose our sense of identity

If we sin, a sense of failure can quickly make us lose our new sense of spiritual identity. We start thinking of ourselves as sinners again. This leaves us weak and it becomes a self-fulfilling prophecy. Instead, if we fall, we should assert

---

[126] Romans 7:7.

repeatedly that sin is now just a depersonalized, left-over force within us. It is no longer our identity. "It is no longer I who live, but Christ who lives in me…" It is no longer I who sin.

(ii) A sense of rejection demoralizes us

A wrong focus on the Law can leave us feeling rejected by God, especially if we slip. With that terrible weight on our back, we lose heart. Instead, a heartfelt "sorry" quickly restores our sense of fellowship.[127] We can't undo our sins. But "sorry" means we immediately re-align ourselves with Christ's rejection of sin and his life of the Spirit. It doesn't matter how often we have to say it…[128]

Guilt is the devil's great lie and is the source of his power over us through Law. But "There is now therefore no condemnation" – *ever*![129]

---

[127] This is for those who are already Christians. *Sorry* is not the same as asking for forgiveness. It is simply saying that you regret allowing something to block your experience of fellowship with God. You repent of it by saying sorry. Of course, you have to mean it. This is not a cheap formula. But this act of will instantly restores the power of the Spirit in your life by showing that you disown sin. (At initial conversion, new believers of course need to pray for forgiveness.)

[128] Matthew 18:22.

[129] "You must never go back 'under the law'. You must really learn to say, 'There is therefore now no condemnation to them that are in Christ Jesus'… Whatever you may feel about yourself, and whatever you may know to be true about yourself, 'there is now no condemnation'… None! You must not think of yourself and your life in that way." M. Lloyd-Jones Romans 7 Commentary, p 50.

Paradoxically, the more sensitive our conscience, the deeper and harder we can fall, with the devil on our back, so that as Jesus enigmatically said, the state of someone who has been cleansed can become "worse than his first state."[130]

(iii) We stop seeing the Law as personal

Our Christian life is about a loving relationship with God. If we begin to see Law as an impersonal set of moral standards, it becomes unfulfilling, and the easier to break. But if we realize that what we do or don't do will please or displease God personally, then the Law is what it should be: a code of love.[131] But focusing on the Law as a set of moral standards rather than on our heavenly relationship, will leaves us more prone to sin.

(iv) We lose our spiritual enjoyment

If our new-found delight in fellowship with God becomes replaced with dry moralism, we lose the excitement of life in the Spirit.[132] Our Christian life becomes less satisfying. Then the

---

[130] Luke 11:26. Cf. 2 Peter 2: 20.

[131] Cf. "Do not grieve the Spirit" Ephesians 4:30.

[132] The ethos and preaching in many churches, alas, has much to answer for in this regard.

door is left open for temptation to find satisfaction outside God's ways. The joyless letter of the Law leaves us vulnerable to this.

(v) We stop focusing on future rewards – only on Law's demands

A weekly diet of demands in church to "be better and try harder", without emphasizing our future rewards, will leave us uninspired. As motivation wanes, we will find ourselves increasingly struggling to meet the standards we hear about.[133] Then we can slip into the downward spiral described above.

Guilt, rejection, lack of love, lack of joy, lack of hope, all these things will leave us reacting badly to the letter of the Law and give sin extra strength in our lives. It is an unholy cocktail that uses something holy for our undoing.

But before we leave this subject, let us focus for a moment longer on the dire role of guilt in this problem of life under Law without Spirit. It is a serious problem in far too many Christians' lives.

A sense of guilt brings a feeling of rejection. All human beings (since Eden) are naturally prone to this sickness. With some, it takes hold of their lives with demonic

---

[133] See Part 4 below for the importance of Hope in the Christian life.

destructiveness. But even as mature Christians, one failure can knock us off balance – unless we quickly reassert our identity and bathe in God's fatherly love.

An unchecked sense of guilt creates a spiral. If we fail, we feel bad about not meeting God's standards and we begin to lose sight of our wonderful new Christian identity. We try harder to reform ourselves, but we have already begun to see ourselves as sinners, and so of course… we fail again.

Things get worse. Driven by the resulting sense of lack of self-worth, we might run wildly in the opposite direction, doing anything we can to compensate for the huge emotional need we feel in our lives.[134]

This deepens the cleft even more between what we know is right and how we are living. The resulting psychological turmoil is why some people end up abandoning their Christian profession. Deep down they feel like failures, wretched and rejected. They lose enjoyment, give up trying, and naturally seek all the more to fill the huge hole in their lives in other ways.

This is why the Law without Spirit leads to a struggling Christian life.

---

[134] This spiral of guilt and confusion is why teenagers can sometimes shock their parents (and themselves) by their behaviour, as they grapple with realigning relationships and standards in their changing world.

But –

> " Sin will have no dominion over you because you are not under Law, but under grace."[135]

And –

> "To set the mind on the Spirit is life and peace."[136]

It is worth noting pastorally, in conclusion, that a sense of rejection from people around us can also trigger off a spiral of lack of self-worth. If we don't counteract this by finding daily delight in God's passionate embrace, we can end up compensating with a morbid self-love. The resulting self-indulgent actions may then seem to be anything but a concern for Law. But if our motivation is to counteract an inner sense of worthlessness, that is exactly where we are – back under Law: judging ourselves as inadequate by a perceived set of standards.

Instead of seeing ourselves as inferior – in the eyes of God or of man – we must always see ourselves as dignified children of God, because of his work in our lives. We are holy royalty... princes and princesses.

This is the radical, powerful, and irrevocable Good News:
> "The old has passed away. Behold the new has come."[137]

---

[135] Romans 6:14.

[136] Romans 8:6.

[137] 2 Corinthians 5:17.

The need for a healthy diet

Do we experience the sort of victorious living celebrated by Paul in chapters such as Romans 6 and 8; the joyful, peace-filled life of the Spirit described in Galatians 5? Or do we find ourselves struggling like the "wretched man" in Romans 7?

Is the problem that we are sometimes weaker than we should be because we are undernourished? We haven't been getting enough proper food. We don't focus enough on the great central truth of transformational righteousness by the Spirit.

If we don't, we can end up slipping back under the influence of Law without realizing it. Church preaching and the sort of hymns we sing can even contribute to this.[138]

It is good and right (of course) to celebrate the fact that God has shown great mercy by forgiving our guilt. But the way some churches almost exclusively emphasize forgiveness of sins, it seems as if this were the whole story rather than only the prelude.

---

[138] *Most of the hymns we have sung over the centuries have been sin-centred hymns, and most sermons are designed to make us feel guilty by pointing out how far short we fall. I believe that most churchgoers feel holiest when the feel guilty; in fact they would feel it was presumptuous not to feel guilty.* Derek Prince, By Grace Alone, p 133.

The glorious end result of it all is that we are back where we belong, in God's family. The Cross is not the reason for God's forgiveness. It is the result of it. It demonstrates it. It enacts it. It brings us deliverance. It is God's merciful plan of escape into life in his Kingdom.

In church, do we give enough emphasis to our changed life and our hope of glory? What about the songs we sing? Do we sing about the Cross as the powerful victory over sin and darkness – or do we only, or mainly see it as a punishment for guilt.

After discussing divergent views of the Atonement in Mere Christianity, C. S. Lewis graciously points out that whatever theory you hold about *how* it works, the most important thing is to believe that it does work.[139] He uses the analogy of a person who needs a good meal: he can eat and benefit from it even if he understands very little about how it does him good.

Up to a point he is right. To believe in God's forgiveness is infinitely better than not believing it.

But using this food analogy, I'd like to go a little further. Modern food science *can* help us make choices that ensure we eat properly and are stronger in the long run. We know that we can't live healthily on an exclusive diet of

---

[139] Mere Christianity, Book Two, Chapter 4, p 59.

hamburgers. And even something wholesome like potatoes or pasta won't do on its own. We need the balance.

I think that a theory of Atonement which has insisted on the central place of "justification" meaning the forgiveness of guilt, can deflect our focus from the more vigorous, positive message of spiritual transformation through the Cross.[140]

> **"If anyone is in Christ he is a new creation. The old has passed away. Behold the new has come."**[141]

A gospel which emphasizes "justification" as the forgiveness of guilt, has undoubtedly given hope and comfort to many Christians. Its message of having our slate wiped clean is indeed a gospel of grace.

But a message of forgiveness is only the start of the Good News. And in our daily living, a focus on guilt – even guilt forgiven – might lead us back under Law in subtle ways long-term unless it is balanced by the rest of the message.

If the emphasis in our churches is on our being *sinners*

---

[140] One of the most blatant examples I have seen is the translation of "made righteous" in a Spanish Bible as *"ser libre de culpa"*. This is a narrow interpretation which *seems* to be a positive message but establishes a negative focus from the outset. It is not strong enough as the basis for our Christian life.

[141] 2 Corinthians 5:17.

– forgiven yes, but sinners still – such a message is less than half the story. In Protestantism we don't believe enough in our changed identity. One sign of this is that we are always asking for forgiveness that has already been given, once and for all.

Such a one-sided emphasis undermines the power of the Good News in transforming us, so vital for a strong, daily Christian life. We can end up focused on the letter of the Law and our shortcomings.

To know that our sins have been forgiven is the beginning of precious Good News to be thankful for.

To know that we are spiritual royalty in God's holy family, now and forever, is so much more.

Meditations

Heart transplant

Postcard from Israel – the Beauty of Holiness

The Light from Behind the Sun

Meditations

Heart Transplant

We have had a change of heart....

We were dying, and we've been given a new lease of life.

You could say we've had a spiritual heart-transplant.

Just as the weak patient's donor-heart starts pumping fresh life around body and mind, our new donated heart fills us with spiritual life. We are new people. It's the heart of Jesus that beats in us now.

Not that we cease to be ourselves. We are individuals, with all our uniqueness, and always will be. Sometimes the bold statements of the New Testament can make us think that somehow we lose our individuality: "It is no longer I who live but Christ who lives in me."

But the new heart from Jesus helps us to be our true selves, to reach our unique God-given potential.

We can be just like the man who has been given a new

lease of life; we can go out and live life to the full. We've been given a second chance.

But there the analogy ends.

For the patient with the new donor-heart will die.

The heart of Jesus in us gives us life that never ends.

Meditations

Postcard from Israel – The Beauty of Holiness

In the northernmost part of Israel, on the border with Syria and Lebanon, there is a place called Dan. It is the ancient site of Jeroboam's altar, which has now been excavated and stands there as a shameful reminder (said our Jewish tour guide) of the ugliness of adultery against God.

Just a few minutes' walk away, you come across the rushing, crystal-clear waters that spring from Mount Hermon on their way to filling the River Jordan – God's providence, and Israel's lifeline to this day. Trekking across that rugged, arid terrain, and standing there under the baking heat of Israel's Middle Eastern sun, you could be forgiven for thinking that this is one of the loveliest sites you will ever see.

The contrast made me think of that phrase: "the beauty of holiness."

To be honest, I had always found it difficult to sing words like "Holy, holy, holy, Lord God Almighty" with much enthusiasm. It left me a little cold. I had to re-examine what I understood was meant by holiness. When people have tried to explain it with notions of "otherness", being "set apart" or clinical morality, it can seem uninspiring and cold.

... Until we remember that the heartbeat of the Law is love. The "beauty of holiness" is the beauty of God's life itself, in all his dazzling perfection and loveliness.

This is what God was trying to instil in his people in his marriage covenant with them at Sinai. He was not like any other god. His breath-taking perfection made him uniquely special. His awesome flawlessness set him apart from all the uncleanness that people were used to in this fallen world. This was how he wanted to be known, if they were going to stay in a relationship with him. He will not accept anything less. And holy was how he wanted his own people to be also – to be like him.[142]

So let's think of holiness in Paul's positive words as

> "whatever is true, whatever is noble, whatever is right, whatever is pure, whatever is lovely, whatever is admirable – anything excellent or praiseworthy…"

Holiness is the life-giving blessing of those lovely, crystal-clear waters gushing from Mount Hermon.

Holiness is the perfect, glorious Spirit of God.

"There is a river whose streams make glad the city of God."[143]

---

[142] Jesus re-emphasized God's eternal standards when he told his disciples to "be perfect" like their heavenly Father.

[143] Psalm 46:4.

Meditations

The Light from Behind the Sun

Every day, we have a purpose in living – a clear and powerful calling that gives each day fulfilment. It is the same calling for all of us; it never changes, regardless of our circumstances. Put in the simplest terms: our daily purpose is to love and do good.

This is the heartbeat of God. It is what life is all about. We can embrace this calling anytime anywhere. We don't need to look for it, pray for it, or wait for it.

Sometimes we let life get too complicated, even church life and our theology. But this truth is simple and couldn't be easier to put into practice day by day: love God and do good to those around us.

Pursuing this may take us far afield. But equally, it is as simple as saying a positive word to a neighbour, hugging a family member, doing a good job for our boss, or giving a helping hand and a kindly smile to someone in need.

It has been said that human beings want three things in life for deepest happiness: a job to do, someone to love, and a cause to believe in. This is precisely what is on offer through our divine calling, regardless of our circumstances.

Whether we are unemployed or paid, rich or poor, young or old, married or single, we can all embrace this calling every minute of every day, and enjoy deep satisfaction.

By doing good wherever we can, to whomever we can, we tune into God's purposes. We find the meaning of life.

Jesus told us to let our light shine before men. That light is the light of his love in a dark and needy world. God is love. And God is called the Father of Lights. When we walk in his Spirit, we let his life shine into every situation.

Then, to use a phrase from C. S. Lewis, we find ourselves shining with nothing less than *"The Light from Behind the Sun..."*[144]

What a calling to get up and live for every morning!

---

[144] An allusion to Charles Williams' lines in "The Calling of Taliessin" (1944).

PART 4

BRINGING MANY SONS TO GLORY

A Glorious Future

For those whom he foreknew he also foreordained to be conformed to the image of his Son, in order that he might be the firstborn among many brothers. And those whom he foreordained he also called, and those whom he called he also made righteous, and those whom he made righteous he also glorified.[145]

Adam's first and deepest sin was unbelief. He and his wife stopped believing that God was who he was, that God alone had the power and the love to "reward those who seek him".

Our Christian lives now are designed to be the undoing of that great sin. We are called to walk "by faith and not by sight".

But one day everything will be seen as it really is. What a day of unspeakable ecstasy that will be! We can experience a foretaste of it now in many ways. But mostly our rewards await that future fulfilment.

Our daily Christian life has a hidden aspect and a future dimension. This is why Faith is so intimately linked with Hope. Much of what we believe now will be revealed to be

---

[145] Romans 8:29-30.

spectacularly true on some great future day – the Day of the Lord. Then we will enjoy the fullest experience of all that we have been seeking and working for.

> **"Faith is the assurance of things hoped for, the conviction of things now unseen."**[146]

The theme of present realities becoming visible in all their glory one day is a major leitmotif in all the New Testament writings. We need this as an anchor for our souls, to motivate us in our daily living.

> "Beloved, we are God's children now, and what we will be has not yet *appeared*; but we know that when he appears we shall be like him, because we shall see him as he is."[147]

> "Set your minds on things that are above, not on things that are on earth. For you have died, and your life is *hidden* with Christ in God. When Christ who is your life *appears*, then you also will *appear* with him in glory."[148]

> "For I consider that the sufferings of this present time are not worth comparing with the glory that is to be *revealed* to us. For the creation waits with eager longing for the *revealing* of the sons of God. ...we ourselves, who have the first-fruits of the Spirit, groan inwardly as

---

[146] Hebrews 11:1.

[147] 1 John 3:2.

[148] Colossians 3:2.

we wait eagerly for adoption as sons, the redemption of our bodies. For in this hope we were saved. Now hope that is seen is not hope. For who hopes for what he sees? But if we hope for *what we do not see*, we wait for it with patience."[149]

"Though our outer self is wasting away, our inner self is being renewed day by day. For this light momentary affliction is preparing for us an eternal weight of glory beyond all comparison, as we look not to the things that are seen but to the things that are *unseen*. For the things that are seen are transient, but the things that are unseen are eternal."[150]

"…to those who by patience in well-doing *seek* for glory and honor and immortality, he will give eternal life."[151]

We could quote many more passages. This message is all over the New Testament in the most explicit terms.

So why do we hear so little of this in churches?

It is right for us as Christians to focus on the wonderful blessings that we are going to inherit on that future day. We need to desire those blessings – passionately.

We are blessed now of course. Life in countries that have

---

[149] Romans 8:18, 23-25.

[150] 2 Corinthians 4:16-18.

[151] Romans 2:7.

been Christianized for hundreds of years can be a very comfortable context to taste the blessings God promises to the faithful. But even in the most stable, happy Christian lives, choosing life in the Spirit will inevitably mean sacrifices and pain of some sort.[152] There is never enough motivation in this life to keep us completely on track. We also need to be *selfishly* seeking the great blessings ahead.

But is this our motivation?

Do we even feel comfortable with it?

Shouldn't we be doing everything selflessly "for the glory of God" anyway?

When we hear people talking about "doing everything to the glory of God", there is a danger of losing sight of the scriptural balance. God's glory is *our* glory, and any teaching which does not put man at the centre of God's plans (with Christ) is misguided.[153] Preaching selflessness for the sake of "God's glory" may sound pious, but it can leave us

---

[152] Cf. Galatians 5:17.

[153] John Piper's recurrent emphasis in his later books on God working always for his own glory carries this risk – unless you also read his wonderful appeal for true "Christian hedonism" for balance: http://www.desiringgod.org/resource/christian-hedonism. Similarly, in looking at *justification* through N. T. Wright's particular covenantal prism, you may take away the impression that there is not enough focus on Christ's simply stated mission to "save the people from their sins" and "bring many sons to glory". God's plans have always been about Christ and Man (together).

unmotivated and weak. It can sound like God is on some sort of eternal ego-trip.

To help us grasp this properly, we have to understand that God's glory is all about his love. Love is the very essence of his glory – a love shared with Man. God is love, more than he is anything else. Love is his life and the driving force in everything he has ever done.

In the beginning God was a family, full of such wonderful life and love, that the creative spirit of God was almost bursting to share it with other beings. As Sinclair Ferguson puts it, "The creation of a family, with children, is the reason for all of God's activity. This is how he intends to show his glory."[154]

That's exactly what he did. He made new children for his family – to share his blessings, to delight with him in the light of life. Our relationship to him was to be man's life and our glory.

"This is eternal life – that they know thee the only true God."[155]

But to lose this divine relationship through sin would

---

[154] S. B. Ferguson (1989), "Children of the Living God."

[155] John 17:3. In Jesus' prayer we can hear him talk about God's ultimate purposes in terms of restoring and sharing what he had with his Father before the world was made – verses 5, 13, 22-24.

mean death, the loss of everything. Suffering would be a foretaste of the final loss of all blessings.

The positive corollary of that is that for believers now, even the smallest physical, everyday pleasure enjoyed in fellowship with him, is a sign of life, a source of spiritual joy, and a foretaste of the eternal blessings that are ours to come.

> **"You make known to me the way of life, in your presence is fullness of joy; at your right hand are pleasures for evermore."**[156]

A preacher I heard speaking in church was very keen to emphasize the apparently selfless message of the Shorter Catechism: "Man's chief end is to glorify God". But his narrow understanding of what this meant was evident when he felt the need to change the subsequent words to "and enjoy doing it forever" – rather than "enjoy *him* forever." I think this "slip" highlights a major problem in evangelical Christianity.

The sort of teaching that downplays our natural desire for blessing, glory and rewards can undermine our delight in the Lord and may get us back under the influence of the Law as a spiritless and joyless way of life.

Some time ago I heard a clergyman teach a series on the Beatitudes. Except he didn't teach the Beatitudes. He

---

[156] Psalm 16:11.

preached on less than one half of each of them:

> ***"Blessed are the meek, for they shall inherit the earth,"***
> became –
> "~~Blessed~~ ~~are~~ <u>the meek,</u> ~~for they shall inherit the earth~~."

It continued like this week after week:
   "~~Blessed are the~~ <u>pure in heart,</u> ~~for they shall see God.~~"
Glorious, exciting promises were turned into yet more challenges to try harder and be better.

In my view and in my experience, we *will* be better when we are motivated by rewards.

Most well-meaning Christians don't need to be challenged all the time to try harder. What we need is to be *inspired* to be better. We need to be constantly reminded of the amazing rewards ahead:

> **"We shall be like him for we shall see him as he is... Everyone who thus hopes purifies himself, as he is pure."[157]**

To some people this sounds like we are being mercenary. "God does not primarily want us to be happy," said the preacher. "He wants us to be holy." But this sort of teaching sets up a very unhelpful, false dichotomy.

---

[157] 1 John 2:2-3.

"My goal is God himself, not joy nor peace," said a well-meaning hymn. But this sort of approach seems to encourage us to be more holy than Jesus himself –

> "...who for the *joy* that was set before him, endured the cross."[158]

God is our joy – as he was Jesus' joy. He is the source of all our happiness. The rewards of a relationship with him are so great we will give up everything else if we have to.

"Your steadfast love is better to me than life."[159]

We are prepared to give up lesser things because our sights are set on higher rewards. It's not that we choose God instead of blessings. We choose a life of blessings in God, at any cost, rather than a life without him. Because with him all our needs will be met, on all levels.

Here's what C. S. Lewis helpfully has to say about all this:

> If there lurks in most modern minds the notion that to desire our own good and earnestly to hope for the enjoyment of it is a bad thing, I submit that this notion has crept in from Kant and the Stoics and is no part of the Christian faith. Indeed, if we consider the unblushing promises of reward and the staggering

---

[158] Hebrews 12:2.

[159] Psalm 63:3.

> nature of the rewards promised in the Gospels, it would seem that Our Lord finds our desires, not too strong, but too weak. We are half-hearted creatures, fooling about with drink and sex and ambition when infinite joy is offered us, like an ignorant child who wants to go on making mud pies in a slum because he cannot imagine what is meant by the offer of a holiday at the sea. We are far too easily pleased. We must not be troubled by unbelievers when they say that this promise of reward makes the Christian life a mercenary affair. There are different kinds of reward. There is the reward which has no natural connection with the things you do to earn it, and is quite foreign to the desires that ought to accompany those things. Money is not the natural reward of love; that is why we call a man mercenary if he marries a woman for the sake of her money. But marriage is the proper reward for a real lover, and he is not mercenary for desiring it.[160]

There is a selfish element in love (so to speak) which is at the very heart of the experience. The beloved gives us pleasure. The relationship is a source of blessings and delight. That's why we choose him/her. Loving is a rewarding experience. Enjoying the person's love in return is our satisfaction. This motivates us to give up anything that stands in the way of our relationship to God, even to the point of death, if necessary.

The prospect of future glory is everywhere in the New Testament writings. So why do we hear so little about it?

---

[160] The Weight of Glory, pp 26-27.

Why do some clergy even try to play down our desire for it?

When Paul says that by patiently doing good we seek for "glory, honour and immortality" it leaves some people uncomfortable. Is it right to seek glory? Can we not live by *purer* motives?

That is why I heard one church leader switch that verse round to re-focus it on God's glory, not ours. He paraphrased it as "those who seek to glorify God" so as to avoid any sense that we might be seeking self-centred rewards. But that is not what the text says.

Another clergyman touched on the theme of Christian hope one evening. He spoke for 20 minutes about hope, using Biblical verses from the New Testament, but without once mentioning
   - Our future glory
   - The resurrection
   - Our inheritance as children of God

I was left wondering if we were even using the same Bible!

I quote this only to highlight the importance of getting the right Biblical balance in this whole area. When Paul talks of hope, it is nearly always about our astonishing future blessings. That was his driving force. It is also the major motivating theme in the letters of Peter and James, writing to Christians who were facing difficulty.

If the hope of glory was the dominant motivation for great, selfless men of the Spirit like the Apostles, and all the heroes of faith, famous or unnamed, celebrated in Hebrews 11, how can we think that *we* will be strong or successful in our Christian walk if we neglect it? Of the three really important things listed by Paul, Faith, Hope and Love, it seems to me that Hope is the poor relation in churches these days.

I quote from the above episodes very reluctantly, because the church leaders I mentioned are dear brothers, living dedicated lives. But around that period in my later Christian life, I admit I was floundering, like the man in Romans 7. I desperately needed someone to repair my wings, to take me back to the heights that are our proper domain as Christians. I needed more than a weekly challenge to be better. I needed to be inspired again.

So this is my appeal to church leaders everywhere. Don't badger or berate us… Fix our gaze heavenwards and help us to soar.

Hope – A Marginalized Teaching

It might be helpful to explore why the theme of heavenly blessings has become a marginalized one in many churches.[161]

I think we can identify at least three reasons.

(i) Pie in the Sky

In the past, church people have often been accused of being "too heavenly minded to be any earthly use." *Pie in the sky*, and all that… Stung by this caricature, churches today tend to run headlong in the opposite direction.

    C. S. Lewis points out two things about this.
- Firstly, in his experience, it is precisely the people who have been most "heavenly minded" who have acted with the greatest urgency to change this world for the better.
- Secondly, "either there is pie in the sky, or there isn't"! If there isn't then we have all been sold a lie. As Paul says (though admittedly with his record of

---

[161] Poor translations in the NIV don't help! Galatians 5:5 - "For we in Spirit by faith eagerly await the hope of righteousness" (i.e. the hope that is the reward of the righteous) becomes "we eagerly await the righteousness for which we hope". This is a really unhelpful interpretation.

sufferings, his was an extreme case):

> *"If it is for this world only we have hoped, we are of all men most to be pitied."*[162]

We needn't shy away from an emphasis on heaven. It is at the heart of our Christian faith.

(ii) Rewards – a tricky doctrine to handle

If you read Calvin's masterly "Institutes of the Christian Religion" you may get the feeling, as I did, that there is one section where, uncharacteristically, he does not seem at all comfortable dealing with a core Biblical theme. Paul used this theme as a repeated source of motivation and encouragement for believers, but Calvin seems under pressure almost to explain it away.

It is the theme of heavenly rewards.

Of course Calvin treats it.[163] He is too scripturally faithful

---

[162] 1 Corinthians 15:19.

[163] Book Third, Chapter 18. He is very exercised to defend the evangelical core doctrine of grace from any notion that earthly or heavenly rewards are due to good works. So he doesn't feel at ease to offer such prospects to us as motivation. In Chapter 10 however he talks more positively of heaven as our true home, though without emphasizing "rewards" and mainly as a warning not to cling too closely to things of this world.

to do otherwise. But he doesn't bring out the inspiring power of this truth to motivate believers in the way that Paul and the other New Testament writers clearly intended. He doesn't enjoy it in quite the way he does the rest of Christian truth.

Historically the reason for this is obvious. The Roman Catholic church had placed great store by the need for people to live religious lives, linking heavenly blessings with this. But the message had become garbled and led unfortunately to an undermining of the key Biblical principle of salvation by faith.

Luther, Calvin and the other reformers (except Osiander) emphasized instead an inheritance of eternal life based on Christ's merits, understood as something forensic, done and sealed in a quasi-legal credit ledger, rather than (primarily) in our life's substance and experience. Any sense of future rewards being linked to actual righteousness, lived out on earth, ran the risk of leading believers back into Catholic error and away from salvation by faith.

But these were false dichotomies. We *can* receive Christ's righteousness by faith when we are filled with the Spirit, and then proceed to work it out and make it ours in life and experience. In fact we are told to do this.

"If by the Spirit you put to death the deeds of the

flesh you will live."[164]

The Reformers sought to separate "justification" from "sanctification"? This undergirded the notion that we receive external forensic righteousness as something separate from the power that shapes our daily living.

But *justification* and *sanctification* are two different ways to describe our transformed new life – two sides of the same coin.[165] We are made righteous; we are made holy. Both are instantaneous at regeneration. Both are worked out in ongoing daily living. Our holiness and righteousness, received by faith and lived out in experience, form the basis for our eternal rewards. That is the heart of our motivation.

Paul says about this motivation, that we always "aim to please him" –

> **"For we must all appear before the judgment seat of Christ, so that each one may receive what is due for what he has done in the body, whether good or evil."**[166]

---

[164] Romans 8:13.

[165] Whereas Paul often uses the word *righteousness* to explain the blessing we receive from the Blood, the writer of Hebrews almost always uses the terminology of *cleansing, holiness, sanctification* to refer to the same blessing. To be "*sanctified*" means to be made holy. Sanctification is instantaneous – as well as a lifelong experience.

[166] 2 Corinthians 5:10.

In an effort to secure the primacy of "faith alone" the Reformed churches have arguably gone too far in downplaying the importance of righteous living linked to our heavenly rewards. In fact, an emphasis on "rewards" in heaven has been known to infuriate church leaders in the Reformed tradition.[167] (I don't know enough about current Catholic emphases to be able to comment in their case.)

(iii) Our Understanding of Heaven

Meanwhile we all wish our perspectives on heaven's blessings were better informed. We welcome the poetic and allegorical visions of the future Age which we find in Revelation. But without a more concrete understanding of heaven's blessings, we tend to shy away from any emphasis that for example seems in danger of suggesting the possibility of superiority/inferiority within the heavenly family.

Whatever we know or don't know about heaven, something deep inside us tells us that it will not be competitive, with elated winners and less than elated *also-rans*. We have a deep instinct (rightly) that it will not be a place marred by any sense of failure, of being second-best, or sub-standard. We will enjoy perfect bliss with God.

So how can there be different rewards for Christians?

---

[167] William Still relates one such incident following a conference where he spoke on this theme.

Or will our experience of heaven all be the same?

A helpful way to understand this problem is to think of our present experiences within families.

As a father, I love all three of my children equally, and always will. But in any family context, even where members enjoy shared blessings and common experiences, there are also many differences in our personal stories. There are precious moments unique to each relationship. There are whole chapters in our lives where the intersections of our journeys have created wonderful variations reflecting different personalities and pathways.

This is what I think heaven will be like. As Christians, we will have most things in common. We will enjoy a shared inheritance and equal perfection. God loves us equally.

But in addition, we will have unique stories that we delight in sharing with our heavenly Father. This will be our *white stone* with our own secret name written on it.[168] Our individualized relationship with him will be our eternal bliss, and the source of all the blessings that flow from that.

So "whether we are at home or in the body, we make it our aim to please him." Our daily life is a loving walk with a

---

[168] Revelation 2:17.

heavenly father. All the adventures, delights and growing experiences that this brings us will be the stuff of heaven. We will remember it all, and in a sense relive it all with him, in glory forever.

We must live our daily lives with an eye fixed firmly on our future heavenly glory. It is the very essence of our Christian motivation.

> **"I have heard of your faith in Christ Jesus and of the love which you have for all the saints *because of* the hope laid up for you in heaven."**[169]

* * * * * * * * * * * * * *

---

[169] Colossians 1:4-5.

Difficult Texts

We rejoice in our sufferings, knowing that suffering produces endurance, endurance produces character, and character produces hope, and hope does not disappoint us, because the love of God has been poured into our hearts through the Holy Spirit which has been given to us. **Romans 5:3-5**

For we know that if the tent that is our earthly home is destroyed, we have a building from God, a house not made with hands, eternal in the heavens. For in this tent we groan, longing to put on our heavenly dwelling, if indeed by putting it on we may not be found naked. For while we are still in this tent, we groan, being burdened—not that we would be unclothed, but that we would be further clothed, so that what is mortal may be swallowed up by life. He who has prepared us for this very thing is God, who has given us the Spirit as a guarantee. So we are always of good courage. We know that while we are at home in the body we are away from the Lord, for we walk by faith, not by sight. Yes, we are of good courage, and we would rather be away from the body and at home with the Lord.
2 Corinthians 5:1-7

Then two men will be in the field; one will be taken and one left. Two women will be grinding at the mill; one will be taken and one left. **Matthew 24:40-41**

Difficult Texts...

Romans 5:3-5

We rejoice in our sufferings, knowing that suffering produces endurance, endurance produces character, and character produces hope, and hope does not disappoint us, because the love of God has been poured into our hearts through the Holy Spirit which has been given to us.

Some of this passage is immediately clear. We understand how suffering develops our Christian character by drawing faith-based endurance out of us. It is the same process by which Jesus developed and proved himself to the perfect man[170], though from the beginning he was sinless. This is the "discipline" or "training" which the writer of Hebrews says in chapter 12 is painful at present but later yields rewards. (He is not talking there about "discipline " as punishment.)

Ok, that's clear. But how does character "produce hope"? (*"Works hope"* is another possible translation.)

This means that when we make sacrifices for the Kingdom, we are "laying up treasure in heaven". We are adding to our glorious future inheritance (our hope).

---

[170] Hebrews 5:8-9.

Tests of our character add to our heavenly rewards. Gold is proven to be genuine by going through fire, says Peter. When we are faced with challenges in life and choose the path of faith and hope, it will result in our having praise, glory and honour heaped upon us.[171]

We may not always live perfectly, we may not be very consistent, but if faithful living is the general direction of our lives, "great will be our reward in heaven".

As Paul says in another place:

> **"This slight, momentary affliction is preparing for us an eternal weight of glory beyond all comparison."**[172]

Paul then says that this hope of glory "does not disappoint us". It is assured. It is guaranteed.

How do we know?

Paul gives the answer.

Because the love of God has already been shed abroad in our hearts. We already have the spirit of glory within us. That's the guarantee.

---

[171] Romans 2:6-7. *He will render to each one according to his works: to those who by patience in well-doing seek for glory and honour and immortality, he will give eternal life.*

[172] 2 Corinthians 4:17-18

Love is the spiritual essence of our relationship with God. His love is our life and glory. Paul is simply saying that we already have this spirit of glory within us. That's why we can be sure our Christian hope of final glory will be fulfilled.

These spiritual realities can be experienced now, but they will be revealed in their breathtaking fullness on the last day:

> **"I consider that the sufferings of this present time are not worth comparing to the glory that is to be revealed to us. For the creation waits with eager longing for the *revealing* of the sons of God... In this hope we were saved."**[173]

This was "the hope of Israel" for which Paul said he was prepared to be in chains.[174]

---

[173] Romans 8:18-19, 24.

[174] Acts 28:20. Cf. Acts 23:6 and 24:15. Resurrection hope was at the heart of true Jewish faith as the fulfilment of the everlasting covenant with Abraham.

Difficult Texts...

2 Corinthians 5:1-7

For we know that if the tent that is our earthly home is destroyed, we have a building from God, a house not made with hands, eternal in the heavens. For in this tent we groan, longing to put on our heavenly dwelling, if indeed by putting it on we may not be found naked. For while we are still in this tent, we groan, being burdened—not that we would be unclothed, but that we would be further clothed, so that what is mortal may be swallowed up by life. He who has prepared us for this very thing is God, who has given us the Spirit as a guarantee. So we are always of good courage. We know that while we are at home in the body we are away from the Lord, for we walk by faith, not by sight. Yes, we are of good courage, and we would rather be away from the body and at home with the Lord.

Paul is eagerly looking forward to the resurrection. He says it's not that he wants to die (be *unclothed*), but he passionately longs for the glorious freedom from suffering and mortality that will be his when resurrected (i.e. properly *clothed*).

The Spirit we have within us now is the guarantee of that resurrection (verse 5). As Paul says in another place:

> "If the Spirit of him who raised Jesus from the dead dwells in you, he who raised Christ Jesus from the

> **dead will give life also to your mortal bodies, through his Spirit which dwells within you."**[175]

However, there is a complicated section in this passage in 2 Corinthians. It can seem as if Paul is also expecting some intermediate state where he is *bodiless* but "at home" with the Lord (verse 8).

That would be a misreading. He simply means that he is aware of the alternatives: either stay in this world ("away from the Lord", so to speak, though God is always with us) OR leave his present physical state and be "away from the body" so as to enter into the glorified heavenly state – including resurrection.

There is no in-between state for humans. When we die, it is like falling asleep. The next thing we know, we will wake up; the whole night will have passed in what seems like a second. It will seem immediate. And we will be resurrected at that moment when we hear and see Jesus coming back in the clouds with glory and triumph.

The notion that our souls can exist without our bodies, and "go to heaven" after death while we await our bodily resurrection, arises out of a misunderstanding of several so-called "proof-texts".[176] There is also a failure to imagine how

---

[175] Romans 8:11. Cf. Philippians 3:21.

[176] E.g. Ecclesiastes 12:7. See "Home Movies" below for further thoughts.

the worlds of time and eternity relate to each other.[177]

How can our human souls exist without our bodies? And if they can, and even enjoy bliss in Paradise – what is the point of a physical resurrection afterwards? Why do we need it?

One of the clearest passages in the New Testament telling us what happens at the end of the world as we know it, is from Paul's letter to the Thessalonians:

> **"We who are alive, who are left until the coming of the Lord, shall not precede those who have fallen asleep. For the Lord himself will descend from heaven with a cry of command, with the archangel's call, and with the sound of the trumpet of God. And the dead in Christ will rise first; then we who are alive, who are left, shall be caught up together with them in the clouds to meet the Lord in the air; and so we shall always be with the Lord."**[178]

There is no sense in this passage that those who have died before that day are anywhere except in the ground, nor in any state other than dead (= *asleep*). There is not a hint whatsoever that previously glorified, heavenly souls will be reunited with their bodies at that point. We will come back

---

[177] Sometimes we get a little help from sources beyond the Scriptures. The 2014 film "Interstellar" is a wonderful (though unbiblical) exploration of what life could be like beyond the familiar parameters of time and three-dimensional space.

[178] 1 Thessalonians 4:15-17.

to life – pure and simple.

And wonderful....

That will be the end of the universe, and the beginning of a new eternal age. As C. S. Lewis says:

> When that happens, it is the end of the world. ....when you see the whole natural universe melting away like a dream, and something else – something it never entered your head to conceive – comes crashing in; something so beautiful to some of us and so terrible to others that none of us will have any choice left. For this time it will be God without disguise; something so overwhelming that it will strike either irresistible love or irresistible horror into every creature

* * * * * * * * * * * * *

Difficult Texts…

Matthew 24:40-41

Then two men will be in the field; one will be taken and one left. Two women will be grinding at the mill; one will be taken and one left.

There have been many convoluted theories about this so-called "rapture". But the proper scriptural picture is clear to those who know how to see it.

In this teaching, Jesus is primarily emphasizing that life will go on as normal right up to the last minute in earth's history. The Day of the Lord will come as a surprise. That is what he is illustrating when he talks about people doing their ordinary work.

He is also highlighting the separation that will happen. We who are believers, Paul says, will be caught up to join him in the heavens.

> "And the dead in Christ will rise first; then we who are alive, who are left, shall be caught up together with them in the clouds to meet the Lord in the air."[179]

---
[179] 1 Thessalonians 4:16-17

> "Behold, I tell you a mystery; we will not all sleep, but we will all be changed, in a moment, in the twinkling of an eye, at the last trumpet; for the trumpet will sound, and the dead will be raised imperishable, and we will be changed."[180]

All others will be taken away for judgement, whether alive at that point, or raised from their graves:

> "… all who are in the tombs will hear his voice and come out, those who have done good to the resurrection of life, and those who have done evil to the resurrection of judgment."[181]

There will be separation. Both Jesus and Paul emphasize that. But this will be no secret "rapture". This day of resurrection and judgement will be the cosmic, and for some, the all-too-visible end of the age. Paul calls it "the **last trumpet**". All these texts in the Gospels and in Paul's letters clearly fit together. They show a climactic, visible return of Jesus Christ as glorious king and judge, ending the old age, ushering in the new, and dividing the blessed from the rejected.

Nor does Paul give any hint whatsoever that some other supposed "rapture" might precede these eschatological

---

[180] 1 Corinthians 15:51-52.

[181] John 5:28-29.

events he describes clearly in his letters. If there were to have been something prior of this sort, would he not have mentioned it to the Thessalonians in his letter to them, since their future experience in the context of Christ's return was precisely what he was writing to them about?

* * * * * * * * * * * * * *

Other exegetical problems and a plethora of fantastic notions arise when preachers try to tackle difficult apocalyptic chapters in books like Revelation or Daniel and make very basic errors in their approach.

- They don't see the need to get beyond western rationalistic ways of thinking and enter into the mindset of prophetic oriental culture. They expect to find systematic theology in prophecies and scientific empiricism in visions.

- They think too literally. *Three and a half years* may have symbolic significance as half of the perfect number, seven. It almost certainly doesn't carry a literal meaning in predictions, as some have supposed.

- They fail to see that a prophetic vision can simultaneously have two or three layers of application – past, present and future – because in the realm of heavenly truth, there is no time, just one eternal reality. Equally, the same prophecy may apply to personal, national and cosmic contexts using one picture.

- They miss the simple principle that successive visions often refer to the same events, in parallel and from different angles, rather than presenting a linear sequence of different episodes. This is especially the trap in Revelation and Daniel.

- They lose their sense of historical perspective by ignoring the pivotal importance of Israel and the Church in God's interventions in world history.

All this can lead to embarrassing gaffes! There was a time, for example, when much apocalyptic gloom gathered in certain churches as the number of member-states in the European Community approached the Biblical number of 10 (Daniel's Ten Horns). And the connection with Rome made it ominous (Babylon in Revelation). How ridiculous all that seems now that EU membership has risen to 28… with gentle Angela Merkel (at the time of writing) as its leading light!

If we must try to work out historical connections from passages of prophetic apocalypse, at least let us keep some sense of historical perspective, taking our bearings from the big-picture story of Israel and the Church.

It cannot be forgotten, for example, that in the entire history of Israel, there has never been a more bloody chapter than the appalling European holocaust of the 1940's. Is that perhaps adumbrated anywhere in Biblical prophecies, linked with that modern-day miracle of Biblical proportions – the return of Israel to its ancient homeland?... You might expect so.

Nor has there ever been a longer-lasting, more virulent global opponent to Christianity than Militant Islam. Think of the once Christian countries in the Middle East and North Africa which are now Islamic. If we are going to try to identify the "Antichrist", we might at least begin to think on that scale.

Even so, it must always be borne in mind that if the world continued say another 1000 years, we can't know how perspectives might have changed by then. Until very recently, Russian Communism seemed to be a threat to Christian civilization of eschatological proportions. At the time of writing, after only 25 years, it is already beginning to seem like a historical blip.

Speaking to a group of IVF students in Scotland, William Still of Gilcomston South Presbyterian Church in Aberdeen, once showed, in his inimitable style, how ridiculously end-time theories pile up on each other when church leaders cannot approach scripture texts with a proper feel for prophecy, not to mention a modicum of spiritual common sense! So-called dispensationalist pre-millennialism is surely the worst:

> "It goes into almost a maze of covenants and dispensations... There are really two second comings, for and with Christ's church, two or three resurrections (if not four), and also three judgements. There are also, as indicated, two peoples of God, Israel on the earth and the Church in heaven, which according to some will be eternally separate."[182]

His advice is always to get our bearings first from the clear passages, and then if we dare, try to work out what is indicated by the obscure ones (e.g. Revelation 20).

> "Certainly one good principle to follow would be for us all to put far more emphasis on the clear passages of Scripture, and not base our case so very much on the difficult, dark and obscure passages."[183]

And one of the clearest texts about the end of time is the passage in Thessalonians, which we have referred to in previous sections:

> **"For the Lord himself will descend from heaven with a cry of command, with the archangel's call, and with the sound of the trumpet of God. And the dead in Christ will rise first; then we who are alive, who are left, shall be caught up together with them in the clouds."**[184]

---

[182] W. Still, (1976). Towards Christ's Coming, p 27.

[183] W. Still, (1976). Towards Christ's Coming, p 12.

[184] 1 Thessalonians 4:16-17.

Any idea that there could be a preliminary "rapture", after which the world could continue as normal, minus its Christian population (!), is far removed from the clear sense of cosmic finality in Christ's dramatic re-entry. The world is not going to miss that trumpet cry! There will be no secret whisking away of the saints.

That cosmic angelic trumpet blast will be the dramatic beginning of a new, eternal age ("we will always be with the Lord"[185]) – not the start of some supposed intermediate period.

As C. S. Lewis memorably said:

> **"When the author walks on to the stage the play is over."**

---

[185] 1 Thessalonians 4:17.

Meditations

Meeting Your Maker

Home Movies

Heavenly Perspectives

Meditations

Meeting Your Maker

I was driving towards a notorious accident *black spot* one rainy winter's evening when I felt a sudden urge to pick up my mobile phone and check for messages. Of all places!... I held myself back (from breaking the law) with the thought, "That's a sure way to meet your Maker!"

The quaintness of that old phrase struck me. It made me smile. Then suddenly the wonder and reality of it shot through me like a burst of heavenly electricity. To be face-to-face with the One who made us... the One for whom we were made. What an explosion of love there will be when *HE* embraces us. That will be our glory.

It's not that we will be meeting someone we don't know, for the first time. We are already walking with him every day. More than that, the Bible tells us that we are already *one* with him. How much closer can you get?

I think therefore it is better to avoid using a phrase which you often hear at the beginning of church services: "Lord, we come into your presence". It begs the question, *"Where have you been the rest of the time?"*

There is a sense in which we can say something like that

as a metaphor. We are approaching a Great King in his Court. We just need to be careful not to slip into a way of thinking that separates God's presence in church from our daily living.

Paul says that we should walk in the Spirit, giving thanks to God all the time and for everything. Love, joy and heavenly peace should shine through in our daily, ordinary situations as we seek to do everything "in Jesus' name".

Heavenly realities remain to some extent hidden now. That is why much of the language used by Biblical writers talks of "appearing" and "revealing". Unless you look very closely, a Christian's weekly engagements can often look just the same as anyone else's.

But there will be that wonderful moment, one day, when we will suddenly see spiritual truths as they really are. The curtain will be pulled back. What dancing there will be then! What feasting, what celebrations!

The hope of seeing God in person is not something we have to vaguely wish for, or wait to see if it actually happens. That is the ordinary meaning of "hope" – but not the Biblical one. Our hope is what we know the future to be.

It is as sure as God is God.

We will see our Maker!

Meditations

Home Movies

Most of us have watched home movies at some time. What nice surprises we get when we look at family videos years later. Forgotten moments relived... We can get such a sense of providence over the years, patterns unfolding, things falling into place, people changing, maturing, growing into what they should be.

This is assuming that when we watch these films we have reached a happy place in life, after relations have developed well, problem periods have been overcome, life has got better and richer. We can even nod wistfully towards the difficult times; we remember the tears; there might be hints of them in the films. But we know the end will turn out well. We are living proof of that.

Heavenly perspectives

Is this what it will be like in heaven, when we look back at the story of Time? We will be able to trace it from beginning to end, for we will be in a world beyond time.

It is hard, perhaps impossible, for us as humans, born in time, to imagine a world where there is none. Because this is so difficult, eternity is often portrayed as endless time – a never-ending sequence of years. But it is a "place" without time. An Endless Present.

This is why Jesus says, "Before Abraham was, I am." He can use two different frameworks of reference. It defies earthly laws of experience, science, and even grammar.

I believe it is why Jesus was able to say to the dying criminal, "Today you will be with me in Paradise". Two thousand years later, the Resurrection still hasn't taken place. But in another world, it is already history. The thief is there, as Jesus promised, resurrected with him. So are we. We haven't reached the Last Day yet in our world's timeline. But in another world, we are already in Glory – watching the story of our lives play out.[186]

Cross-Overs

It is God's rule that the two worlds stay separate. You can't physically break into your home movie and change what happened back then. That is technically not possible. With God it is morally not possible. It is against his rules.

---

[186] This why the writer of Hebrews is able to say that believers have come to God's "mountain" where perfection has been attained (the spirits of righteous men, resurrected). It may also help explain that enigmatic passage in Matthew which talks of the tombs being opened and some of the dead appearing in Jerusalem. If this was not a) a prophetic vision or b) a prediction of the Last Day, it could have been a similar experience to what happened on the Mount of Transfiguration – an exceptional permission by God for some who have entered eternal rest beyond resurrection in history, to enter briefly back into the world of time for the encouragement of believers.

What happens when there is an exceptional interaction of the two worlds? We get a glimpse of it when Samuel is drawn out of his "rest" back into the world of human troubles, by Saul. (Samuel is described as a spirit – that surely means he had a spiritual body, he wasn't a ghost.) This was a black mark against Saul. It wasn't right to even attempt this.

It happened again when Moses and Elijah appeared with Jesus on the hillside. These weren't disembodied spirits. In another world they had already attained their resurrection – though in our world's timeline the Resurrection was still a future event. Elijah and Moses had spiritual bodies, glorified; but just for a moment, they were allowed to break into the past and make an appearance in their own (and our own!) movie.

By contrast, when the "rich man" after his death – evidently after the Day of Judgement – begs Abraham to send someone back to warn his family, the answer is No! It is not allowed.[187]

Towards a Happy Ending

We are surrounded every day by a host of heavenly witnesses, as the writer of Hebrews tell us. They are watching us, cheering us on.

I'm there, smiling. So are you – just as you might realize,

---

[187] Luke 16:19-31.

during a moment's filming on the beach, that one day you will be able to look back at that very moment from a future perspective.

This insight shouldn't undermine the importance of what we do day by day, here and now. You can only look back at what was real. It all has to happen for the story to unfold. We are still making our video by how we live each day. We have full editorial control of it.

We have only one life on earth. We have to make every day count by making the best choices we can, using every minute, every hour to be the best that God helps us to be.

Then we will look back with glowing hearts.

* * * * * * * * * * * * * * *

Meditations

Heavenly Perspectives

Sometimes we go through life with wrong perspectives. If we do, we can end up being impressed by the wrong things. That is a great pity.

Take the size of the universe, for example. Its unimaginable scale can leave us dumbstruck. But to God, a galaxy is the same size as a rock – neither big nor small. He is outside the laws of physics, because he made them. The real miracle is that he made all these things out of nothing. (That is power!) To him the stars of all the galaxies are no more and no less of a challenge than the myriad sub-atomic worlds crammed into one boulder.

God doesn't share our sense of size. It is the same when we think of human achievement. What impresses people on earth must sometimes seem sad from a heavenly perspective – even laughable.

But there is one scale where we can align our human measurements to the divine. It is the scale of Love. Size does matter to God: the size of our hearts – the length and breadth and depths and heights of Love.

Once we accept this, we begin to understand that

- The traffic warden doing his job faithfully every week, because of his relationship with God, is greater than Alexander (the Great).

- The tired, housebound mother devoting herself to a needy baby, her human love infused with the divine, will be more famous than Cleopatra….

Their heavenly rewards will show it.

> "Many that are last will be first."

On the Last Day we'll know – if ever there was any doubt – that all that mattered, all along, was Love.

PART 5

CONTENTMENT

Daily Contentment

"Come to me and let me come in to you and let me come down and sit at your kitchen table, and let's wash the dishes together, and let's go to work together and come home together and do everything together." That God should come in to us at all is beyond our imagining, but that he should want to live our ordinary lives with us and go to work with us tomorrow morning, I do not begin to understand it, but I just know it is true.[188]

Enjoy the Moment

While we are looking forward expectantly to glorious life after Jesus' return, what should be our attitude to the often humdrum daily demands of ordinary living now – including work, for example, which takes up so much of our time?

Firstly let me say that whoever coined the phrase "work-life balance" has done us all a disservice. By implication, it reinforces the idea that work is something to be got out of the way so that we can enjoy proper "life". It is not a helpful antithesis.

But this is the attitude of so many people who are "living

---

[188] W. Still. Theological Studies, pp 109-110.

for the weekend" or for the holidays. It's a great pity.

It is true that since the Curse of Genesis 3, our human work has had an element of hardship, sweat and toil. But for those of us who are walking with God, his blessing can surely make a big difference to work and to every other aspect of our lives. He won't completely undo the effects of the curse in this life – he *can't* without giving us resurrection bodies and creating a new earth – but the Bible is full of promises of peace and prosperity for those who walk in the ways of wisdom.

Finding contentment in the ordinary things of life is the central theme of a much misunderstood book in the Bible: **Ecclesiastes**. The writer of that enigmatic piece of wisdom acknowledges the fallen state of our world – sometimes in the bleakest terms (*vanity of vanity*) – and tells us repeatedly we cannot essentially change it (*Whatever has been done will be done... What gain has the worker from his toil?*)

But although this seems to tempt him initially to despair, he concludes that there is a simple solution. The only way to live contentedly is to *accept* the present limitations, and on that firm basis find satisfaction in the ordinary everyday things of life as we walk in wisdom.[189] He teaches us to enjoy

---

[189] Vanity, contentment and wisdom are major complementary themes in this book. They hold well together if we understand the overall framework. Many commentators can't, and they end up talking about the Preacher "playing a role" (as a materialist), but then find themselves having to admit weakly that he "drops his mask" when he intersperses traditional Jewish wisdom. Kidner (1976) is typical

the blessings of God here and now, just as they are. The key to contentment is to accept the fact that we are not (yet) in a perfect world, but we can walk with God through all its ordinariness and even enjoy it.

> **"There is nothing better for a man than that he should eat and drink, and find enjoyment in his labour. This is from the hand of God...."**[190]

It is notable that to illustrate his point clearly, the writer of Ecclesiastes (the *Preacher*) focuses mainly on work, along with the simple everyday necessities of eating and drinking. He doesn't deny that there will be moments of ecstasy and many exciting surprises in life. But he teaches us to start by finding pleasure in the ordinary things most of us can easily access every day.[191]

If we can do that, we have learned a lot. Work can be a tiresome challenge to many people, but instead, the Preacher urges us to enjoy our work in God's presence. Food and drink are so ordinary that we often take them for granted; but instead they should be a daily cause for gratitude. As

---

of this approach. Eaton (IVP 1983) is nearer the mark, but still sees the book as an attack on "secularism" rather than an encouragement to contentment through spiritual realism.

[190] Ecclesiastes 2:24

[191] He mentions the blessing of marriage, but not as often as work, food or drink, because (a) most people would have no problem seeing this as one of life's most enjoyable blessings; and (b) it is not a universal experience.

should all our daily blessings.... Constant, joyful thanksgiving should be a way of life for the believer.

This thankful lifestyle will help us taste how life was in the very beginning, before the separation between man and God.

Adam was made a spiritual-physical being: not one or the other, but both. Man's spirit, along with God's, was fused with every physical molecule of oxygen in his blood, every nerve in his fingertips, every thought and action and feeling. Material pleasures were simultaneously spiritual experiences. Every moment of earthly life was a celebration of a heavenly relationship with God. Life was heaven on earth.

We must try now to regain something of this initial blessing. What we enjoy will be a foretaste of the perfect world to come. But we must always remember that God's promises have ultimate fulfilment in the Resurrection. We can't have heaven on earth yet. But our lives are "hidden with Christ in heavenly places". We have to live within this dualism.

This is why Ecclesiastes daringly tells us "not be religious overmuch". We shouldn't live as if we were expecting perfect blessings this side of heaven. We can and should expect a lot,[192] and we're encouraged to, in many places in

---

[192] Especially in countries that have long been Christianized.

the scriptures. God will bless us to the uttermost. But sometimes it is a question of timing. This is perhaps the mistake that extreme "prosperity teachers" make. They are right that we should expect the greatest blessings from God in all respects (including health and finances). But sometimes we may have to wait. And for some promises we will have to wait until the resurrection.

The Bible often helps us to get our balance by offering polar extremes, both of which we need to embrace wholeheartedly. This is the holistic Hebrew way of thinking about life – not *either-or* but *both-and*. So, on the one hand Paul urges us to long for the blessings of the Day of the Lord and to live with that as our dominant motivation. On the other hand Ecclesiastes tells us how to live contented lives here and now.

Ecclesiastes is a valuable complement to scriptures which focus our minds on the coming age. Future blessings are not what the writer was inspired to write about in that book, and it causes problems for some Bible teachers. But the *Preacher* does have a bold message about *this* life, as we wait for the revealing of higher realities. He is not contradicting Biblical teaching on hope. He is balancing it with another focus.

The writer arguably does point us forward implicitly to the perfections of the coming age, by stressing the limitations of this age. But it is a subtle approach, and the book's teasing complexity has caused headaches for many a commentator.

A further challenge for people reading Ecclesiastes is that they find it hard to marry the Preacher's apparent materialistic pessimism in some chapters with his godly call to wisdom and contentment in others. There seem to be internal contradictions. But that is the enigmatic, elusive beauty of his wisdom. It is no contradiction. Paradoxically the writer offers a solid basis for a contented lifestyle by giving us one of the Bible's strongest negative doses of realism about life on this earth:

- Life is marked by often chaotic unpredictability ("time and chance happen to all men")
- We live with a sense of ephemerality, because even the surest of earthly blessings will be lost when we die. (It was never meant to be like that.)
- In everything, there is a profound existential emptiness, a sense that things are not as they should be, and that they can never be as fulfilling as they would be if heaven and earth were still fused together as at the beginning.[193]
- Meanwhile there is nothing we can do to change the essential nature of the world ("There is nothing new under the sun"). There can be no deep

---

[193] This is the reason for the great opening sigh of Chapter 1. The problem is not that things are meaninglessly repetitive (a common misreading), but that they are repetitively *meaningless*.

transformation of the way things are.[194]

Against this realistic backcloth, the righteous man can expect God's blessing to make a difference, albeit not total. We can focus on enjoying ordinary daily pleasures with God, even if life is not always an exciting roller-coaster. There will be highs in life for all of us – hopefully many. But the realism of Ecclesiastes helps us enjoy our present lot, no matter how humble or imperfect it appears at times.

Living in such a way as to enjoy the present moment may seem to be at odds with the focus on our heavenly future, encouraged so strongly in other books of the Bible. But this apparent tension disappears when we realize that the Present is our introduction to Eternity, our foretaste of timeless glory. C. S. Lewis puts it beautifully:

> " (he)… destines them to eternity. He therefore, I believe, wants them to attend chiefly to two things, to eternity itself, and to that point of time, which they call the Present. For the Present is the point at which time touches eternity. Of the present moment, and of it only, humans have an experience analogous to the experience which [God] has of reality as a whole; in it alone freedom and actuality are offered them. He would therefore have them continually concerned either with

---

[194] This is the meaning of another misunderstood passage (*a time to die, a time to mourn* etc). It is not meant as comforting lyrical poetry but rather as a stark call to realism. "Everything is beautiful" or "right" in its time means that everything has its inevitable place in man's story; we cannot substantially change the way the world works. So "What gain has the worker from his toil?"

eternity or with the Present – either meditating on their eternal union with, or separation from, Himself, or else obeying the present voice of conscience, bearing the present cross, receiving the present grace, giving thanks for the present pleasure."[195]

* * * * * * * * * * * * * * * * * * * *

In the meantime, our daily moments are not only a taste of the eternal. They are also shaping our eternity in all sorts of wonderful ways.

So we must never despise the ordinary – or see a divide between secular and religious. Church meetings are important times for encouragement and recharging our spiritual batteries. But they should always be seen as preparation for ongoing fellowship with God as we walk through the week ahead. That is where God will be with us, day to day.

Changing a nappy in God's presence can be as spiritual an experience as singing a Wesley hymn. Enjoying a good book or a funny film in cosy communion with our Father can be preparation for heaven as much as preaching the gospel on a cold street corner.

Whatever we do, we must do it in a spirit of faith – always with an eye heavenwards. That is what pleases

---

[195] Screwtape Letters, No 15, p 57.

God.[196] Losing faith was Adam's original sin. Living by faith is our calling now. It is faith that inspires love.[197]

Jesus lived as a man for thirty years of ordinary life in a primitive, obscure village, before embarking on his great teaching mission. He did no miracles during that time. His glory was hidden. He worked, and ate, and slept, and prayed, and waited…. Although he was divine, he lived as a man entirely by faith in his Heavenly Father, as we are called to do. He had to be "made like his brethren in every respect" so that he could redeem our humanity, and glorify it.

Through Jesus' perfect life in us, we get a heavenly foretaste of what it is to enjoy life again under God's love. To be back in God's family. To return to Eden and start again.

* * * * * * * * * * * * * * * * * *

---

[196] Hebrews 11:6.

[197] Galatians 5:6.

Meditations

Kisses from God

Can we praise God while the world falls apart?

Family Holiday

Meditations

Kisses from God

God loves daily fellowship with us…. It's what we were made for.

How disappointed must the Lord have been when he came to the Garden and found that his friends – his new family – were not there for him? How heart-broken was he to find that they had given themselves, instead, to his enemy? How unspeakably tragic.

But Jesus has given us the power to "walk in the Spirit", and when we do, we enjoy constant fellowship with him and our Father. Just as in the beginning, every daily pleasure becomes something to relish with him; every act of providence is a warm touch of his love; every material blessing, a spiritual kiss from God.

What he wants from us, in return, is a heart brimming over with loving gratitude. Whether we are eating, driving, playing, meditating or working, a prayer of thankfulness and joy should always be on our lips, whether voiced, or breathed, or sent heavenwards by a smile.

At the end of the day, issues of sin or holiness are secondary. They are only of importance in so far as they affect our relationship with the Lord.

The only thing that matters in the end is love.

It's what life is all about.

Meditations

Can we praise God while the world falls apart?

On the 26th December 2004, a cataclysmic *Tsunami* was unleashed following an undersea earthquake in the Indian Ocean, killing over 230,000 people in 14 countries. It was the beginning of a year of disasters that left millions suffering or dead. The news on TV or in the papers seemed to be an endless string of reports of misery on a global scale.

A few weeks after the Tsunami, I had the task of leading a worship evening in our church. The question I asked myself and the congregation was: Can we praise God while the world falls apart?

Have you ever had the experience of a niggling voice at the back of your head telling you it is selfish to rejoice in God's blessings while so many people don't even have basics such as food or water? Sometimes a deeper question at the back of our minds is whether God really cares.

There are three answers which might be helpful whenever that inner voice tries to hold us back from celebrating God's goodness.

1. **Firstly, if we didn't thank God for all our blessings, how ungrateful would we be?**

In the story of the ten lepers whom Jesus healed, he expected all of them to come back for a moment of grateful fellowship with him. How disappointed was he that they didn't.

Blessings don't just happen automatically. They are gifts from a person; and when we get a gift, we say *Thank you*. The only right response is appreciation.

If we don't regularly thank God for our salvation, our healing, his provision, our comforts, happiness and health, how ungrateful must that seem to the Lord? *Especially* when there are so many people who can't share these blessings.

In a world that is so needy, when we think of how many blessings we have received from God's hands, how can we do anything other than thank him and be glad?

2. **God *does* care. He paid a terrible price to prove it and reach out to a needy world.**

"Ok," someone says. "But if God blesses some people while others are still suffering, does he really not care about the rest of the world?"

We can be sure that God wants *everyone* to be happy. So badly does he want to rescue men and women from their suffering that he shared it, in its most extreme form. Jesus' terrible death on the cross is the proof we need that God cares. It shows how much God wants to provide a way out of the terrible miseries that have come into the world through Adam's fall.

Let's not forget that human hardships of whatever kind are only a prelude, a foretaste of man's greatest problem – death. In death we lose everything. But God wants everyone to inherit a share in the kingdom of heaven which is eternal and glorious. That is the most important thing. And this offer of abundant life and happiness is open to *everyone*.

Jesus suffered… to put an end to all sufferings.

3. God lets the world run its sad, terrible course because he is waiting, showing mercy.

"Why does God not use his powers meanwhile to intervene and stop the suffering? Couldn't he have prevented the Tsunami?"

There are things that even God cannot do, without undermining himself, contravening his principles in creation and his purposes in redemption.

We know that God would never force men and women to love Him by suspending human free will. He doesn't want robots in his family! Having established this plan with these parameters, when Adam fell, God had to let the whole world fall, with Man, into its current wretched state where millions suffer and die every day – a world which he had intended to be Paradise.

In one of Jesus' parables, a man sows a crop in a field and an enemy comes and sows weeds in with it. "Why don't you just pull out the weeds?" "I can't," is the answer. "Not without uprooting my whole planting. I'll have to wait until the very end and pull everything up together; then we can sort out the weeds and the crop."

That is a picture of how God feels. Until that time, God can only let the world run its course. The weeds and the crop have to grow together.

In C. S. Lewis' classic book, The Problem of Pain, he invites us to think all this through.[198] If God began to interfere with free will and the natural order of things, where would he stop? Could he prevent *all* causes of suffering in the world's natural order? He intends to – but that would mean building a whole new world. Should he stop all humankind from doing anything that inflicts suffering on fellow man? Should he completely overrule everyone's will? What sort of a world would that be? What sort of half-human people would be populating it? It would be a travesty.

The only way God can now *radically* change this fallen, suffering world is to end it, burn it, and create a new one. He is not prepared to do that yet, because he is working to bring more people into his family. Peter tells us we mustn't think of God's waiting as slowness (i.e. not caring). On the contrary, it is a sign of mercy and patience (2 Peter 3:9,15).

---

[198] The Problem of Pain, pp 24-27.

He is constantly reaching out to more and more people to save them.

There will come a final day when he puts an end to all the suffering and creates a new and perfect world. The offer of a share in that amazing kingdom is open to everyone alive today. We can't say that God doesn't care.

* * * * * * * * * * * * * * *

We have three solid Biblical reasons for celebrating God's goodness, even when the world seems to be falling apart.

Meditations

Family Holiday

Have you ever wanted time to stand still? Those moments when pleasure is so sweet, you never want it to end; when circumstances are so perfect you don't want anything to change? If only things could stay exactly the way they are now.

I think this experience gives us a glimpse of what heaven must be like.

Ralph Waldo Emerson said, *"When I read a good book I wish my life were three thousand years long."* He also famously said, *"To fill the hour – that is happiness."*

This absorbing enjoyment of the Present is a goal which the book of Ecclesiastes holds out to us, as we walk in God's blessing:

> *"... for he will not much remember the days of his life because God keeps him occupied with joy in his heart."*[199]

I most regularly get that feeling on family holidays. For me, it is a foretaste of heaven.

Heaven must be an Endless Present, not a never-ending

---

[199] Ecclesiastes 5:20.

sequence of years. It is an ever-unfolding state of bliss; so full and deep it will never be anything other than perfect; interactive and ever developing – yet complete, and in a sense, never-changing.

It is very hard for us – probably impossible – to imagine life without Time. We have grown up in a world where Time is one of the fundamental facts of existence. But we do get inklings of timelessness in those experiences of deep, present contentment, when everything just seems right; when we are floating blissfully free from the past and the future. The Present then seems all that we could want or ever need. As C. S. Lewis says so well in his Screwtape Letters (15):

> "... *the Present is the point at which time touches Eternity.*"

But if we as humans were always destined for an eternal world, why was Adam first placed in a world bound by time?

It seems that our earliest forefathers were destined to live on earth for 1,000 years. As sin established its hold on the human race, this mark was emphatically missed and life-spans fell short of it (Genesis 5). As time went on, and events dramatically changed the environment – and presumably our genetic health – human life began to average at around 70 years.

What was initially meant to happen after a thousand years of life on earth? If death was never part of the original plan, where would Adam and his family have gone once they reached that (1000 years) age of fulfilment? Would they still be with us today?

Would they not perhaps have been transported into a higher, heavenly, timeless world – without dying? Like Elijah, who was transported away in his chariot (2 Kings 2:11)? Is that also what happened to Enoch who "walked with God" until the day God took him away – and suddenly "he was not" (Genesis 5:24)?

Man's earthly years were simply meant to flow into the transcendent, heavenly zone; into an ever-deepening, yet always complete and perfect experience of God and his purposes. Man was meant for timeless Heaven.

We get tastes of Paradise now, when eternity seems to touch the present moment; when God's peace and joy are present to overflowing in surrounding circumstances, and in our hearts. This is when we want Time to stand still. Just like on the best family holiday....

Let's look for those eternal moments. Let's seek ways every day to experience God's timeless Shalom. Let's feed off these experiences to strengthen our hope of a better world, where pleasures are perfect; where blissful contentment and love is all we will ever know.

Heaven will be the ultimate Family Holiday.

* * * * * * * * * * * * * * *

References and Further Reading

Althaus, P (1920). Osiander und Luther, in: Theologisches Literaturblatt 41.

Berkhof, L. Systematic Theology (1941, reprinted 1988). Edinburgh: Banner of Truth Trust.

Brother Lawrence. The Practice of the Presence of God. Trans Delaney, J. J. (1977). New York: Image Books.

Calvin, J. Genesis, in The Geneva Series of Commentaries. Trans. J King (1847, reprinted 1984). Edinburgh: The Banner of Truth Trust.

Calvin, J. Institutes of the Christian Religion. Trans. Henry Beveridge (1949). London: James Clarke & Co Ltd. (Two volumes.)

Ferguson, S. B. (1989). Children of the Living God. Edinburgh: Banner of Truth Trust.

Grudem, W. (1994). Systematic Theology. Leicester (UK): Inter Varsity Press with Zondervan (Michigan, US).

Hauke, R (1999). Gott-Haben – um Gottes Willen. Andreas Osianders Theosisgedanke und die Diskussion um die Grundlagen der evangelisch vestandenen Rechtfertigung. Frankfurt am Main: Peter Lang GmbH.

Lewis, C. S. (1940). The Problem of Pain. New York: Harper-Collins edition, 2001.

Lewis, C. S. (1942). The Screwtape Letters. London: Harper-Collins.

Lewis, C. S. (1949). The Weight of Glory. New York: Harper Collins. (2001 edition.)

Lewis, C. S. (1950). The Lion, the Witch and the Wardrobe. New York: Macmillan.

Lewis, C. S. (1952). Mere Christianity. New York: Touchstone edition 1996.

Lloyd-Jones, M. (1971). Romans. Exposition of Chapter 5. Edinburgh: Banner of Truth Trust.

Lloyd-Jones, M. (1972). Romans. Exposition of Chapter 6. Edinburgh: Banner of Truth Trust.

Lloyd-Jones, M. (1973). Romans. Exposition of Chapters 7:1 – 8:4. Edinburgh: Banner of Truth Trust.

Lloyd-Jones, M. (1974). Romans. Exposition of Chapters 8:5–17. Edinburgh: Banner of Truth Trust.

Luther, M. The Bondage of the Will. Trans. J. I Packer and O.R. Johnston, 1957. Cambridge: James Clarke and Co. Ltd.

Macleod, D. (2014). Christ Crucified. Understanding the Atonement. Nottingham: Inter-Varsity Press.

Marshall, H. (2008), in Tidball, D., Hilborn, D., and Thacker, J. (eds). The Atonement Debate. Papers from the London Symposium on the Theology of Atonement. Grand Rapids (Mi): Zondervan.

O'Kelley, A. (2014). Did the Reformers Misread Paul? A Historical-Theological Critique of the New Perspective. Milton Keynes: Paternoster.

Piper, J. (1993). The Justification of God. Grand Rapids (Mi): Baker Academic.

Piper, J. (2007). The Future of Justification. A Response to N. T. Wright. Wheaton (Il): Crossway Books.

Prince, D. By Grace Alone, edited by Derek Prince Ministries (2013). Bloomington (Min): Chosen Books.

Still, W. (1976). Towards Christ's Coming. Aberdeen: Gilcomston South Church.

Still, W. Collected Writings of William Still (Vol. 1) Theological Studies (1990). Eds de S. Cameron, N. M. and Ferguson, S. B. Edinburgh: Rutherford House Books.

Wengert, T. (2012). Defending Faith. Tübingen: Mohr Siebeck.

Wright, N. T. (2009). Justification. Downers Grove: IVP.

Wright, N. T. (2014). Messiahship in Galatians. In Elliot, M. W., Hafemann, S. J., Wright N. T. and Frederieck, J. (eds): Galatians and Christian Theology. Grand Rapids: Baker Academic.

WEBSITES

John Piper: www.desiringgod.org
Joseph Prince: www.josephprince.org

BIBLE QUOTATIONS

Quotations are from various translations, including the King James Version, Revised Standard Version and English Standard Version, as well as the author's own.

* * * * * * * * * * * * * *

"This is the voice of the bridegroom and the bride, that is to say, sweet cogitations of Christ, wholesome exhortation, pleasant songs or psalms, praises and thanksgiving… Therefore God loveth not heaviness or doubtfulness of spirit: he hateth uncomfortable doctrine, heavy and sorrowful cogitations, and loveth cheerful hearts. Paul saith: 'Rejoice in the Lord always.' And Christ saith: 'Rejoice because your names are written in heaven.'"
(Martin Luther, Commentary on Galatians)

"We must learn to read deep theology without becoming too heavy and thinking that heaviness and solemnity and lugubriousness have to do with holiness. Holiness has a lightness of touch. Holiness dances – did you know that? – it dances with joy because it has to do with wholeness."
(William Still, Theological Studies, p 131.)

* * * * * * * * * * * * * *

A Bio Postscript From the Author

I have been trying to write this book for a very long time. The truths on these pages have been on my heart and mind for many years, imprinting themselves deeply on my experience as time has rolled on. In a sense, this book has been writing me....

I was very fortunate during my teens and twenties to be a member of an inter-denominational church that embraced a wide range of influences – from German mysticism to systematic theology; from Scottish Presbyterians to ecumenical charismatics. Over the years, my own Reformation studies have proved to be a further reference point; and I always find myself returning to C. S. Lewis.

In this book, I've drawn on what I consider to be the best of all of these influences. Spiritual balance is essential in life and study. I am acutely aware of the power of tradition to create blind spots – and to do so very quickly. I've become increasingly wary of any approach that smacks of being doctrinaire. I find this disturbing, for example, with the recent so-called "New" Perspectives on Paul.

At the end of the day, no matter how scholarly or venerable a theological tradition is, there is always the need to revisit it and probe with spiritual common sense. So I am hoping that others will find it helpful to join with me in doing this *double take*.

"You have a very incisive mind, like a surgeon's scalpel, and if you are not careful you could cut through an artery or two."
(The words of the late William Still of Aberdeen.)

Well…

Let the reader decide.

☺

* * * * * * * * * * * * * *

Bill Brodie is a father, husband, grandfather (young ☺), Presbyterian, linguist, teacher trainer, conference speaker and translator. He lives in Northern Ireland. Recent publications include "The Art of Language Teaching" and "I Become A Beer" on cross-cultural communication. He has been awarded the honour of Chevalier dans l'Ordre des Palmes Académiques by the French Education Ministry, and the Europaurkunde by the German Federal State of Brandenburg.

* * * * * * * * * * * * * *

Feel free to contact the author with comments or questions at: http://reflect.brolancon.com